I AIN'T GOIN' TO JAIL: PARDON ME?

A True Story of Redemption, Invention, and
the Fight for Freedom

by

Hugh Carter

I0520663

Copyright Page for All Editions

© 2025 Hugh Carter

First Edition, 2025

ISBN (Hardcover): [ISBN: 979-8-9995783-2-7]
ISBN (Paperback): [ISBN: 979-8-9995783-1-0]
ISBN (EPUB/eBook): [ISBN: 979-8-9995783-0-3]
ISBN: (EPUB/eBook): [ISBN:979-8-9995783-3-4]
ISBN: (Paperback): [ISBN: 979-8-9995783-4-1]
ISBN: (Hardcover): [ISBN: 979-8-9995783-5-8]
ISBN: (EPUB/eBook): [ISBN: 979-8-9995783-6-5]
ISBN: (Paperback): [ISBN: 979-8-9995783-7-2]

Registration Number TXu 2-506-831
Cover design by ["ChatGPT / Hugh Carter Collaboration"]
Interior layout by [Hugh Carter]

For more information, contact: Hugh Carter Publishing LLC
P O Box 145 Beverly, NJ 08010-9998

hughlcarter.com

Author's Legal Disclaimer

This memoir is a true account based on the author's personal experiences, memories, and reflections.
While every effort has been made to present events truthfully, some names, locations, and timelines may have been altered or reconstructed from memory to protect privacy or enhance narrative clarity.

This book is intended for storytelling, public education, and inspiration. It does not constitute legal, medical, psychological, or professional advice. Readers seeking legal guidance should consult a qualified attorney.

The author, Hugh Carter, has received a full Clean Slate Expungement and an official Executive Pardon from the State of New Jersey. Any mention of past legal matters—including arrest, incarceration, or criminal behavior—is shared solely to illustrate the author's personal growth, redemption, and resilience. No part of this memoir is intended to contradict, challenge, or misrepresent the lawful restoration of the
author's rights.

DEDICATION

This book is dedicated to my family—

those we've lost, those still with us, and those yet to come.

Your blood runs through these pages. Your strength shaped my soul.

To my late mother, Alice Carter-Harris, and my late aunt Estelle Phox, who held the family together through fire and heartbreak.

To my father, Hugh Lovejoy Harris, who left this world too soon but never left my heart.

To my sister, Wetonah Carter, and her beloved children—

Shawn Darnell Carter and Aaron Carter, whose memories live forever,

and Reginald Carter, whose life is a continuing testimony of resilience.

To my late niece, Shadeequah Carter, a beautiful soul and loving mother to Blessing Carter, whose name says it all.

To my nephews—Reginald, Demond, Rayshawn , Justin, Jovan and Daquai Carter, to Kevin Michael and Everton Harris—each of you carries a part of this legacy forward.

To Kevin Brian Harris, a beacon of our family's light.

To my nieces—Kiara Carter and Diamond Carter—and to every child born from this family tree,

May you walk boldly knowing you are the continuation of a powerful story.

To my cousin, brother, and co-creator, Bee Phox,

and to my stepfather Ronald Greene, my guardian angel in life and beyond—thank you for the love that saved me more than once.

This book is not just my story.

It's our story—etched in love, fire, struggle, and redemption.

I carry all of you with me.

Don't block your blessings.

—Hugh Carter

ACKNOWLEDGEMENTS

First and foremost, I thank God— for grace, mercy, and every second chance I didn't know I needed.

I want to thank the U.S. Army—for the many lessons, and for making my life whole again.

I express deep gratitude to the Disabled American Veterans Organization, for their integrity and support.

Thank you to Gearhart Law for their guidance and protection of my invention.
To James Klobucar, thank you for helping me find the right path at a pivotal moment.

To Lisa Ascolese, The Inventress, thank you for believing in me and for managing my project with such vision.

To John Harmon, President of the African American Chamber of Commerce of New Jersey—your powerful letter to the Governor helped change the course of my life.

To my attorney, H. Robert Tillman, thank you for standing by me when it mattered most. To the Honorable Governor Phil Murphy of New Jersey

To the best sister a brother could ask for Wetonah Carter, my Aunt Lucy and Aunt Sylvia Harris-Coles, Uncle Jerome Carter, and all the children of my sister and brothers—especially Everton Harris and his family—your presence and support are my foundation. All of my cousins.

To my supporters everywhere, those who saw past my setbacks and uplifted my comeback—this is for you. Through the storms, the fire, and the darkness, You kept me. You knew my story wasn't over.

To my mother, Alice Carter-Harris, and my stepfather, Ronald Greene—thank you for raising me with love, strength, and discipline. Your sacrifices were the foundation of everything I became.

To my entire family, living and departed, thank you for carrying me through each chapter of life:
Wetonah, Reginald, Aaron, Shawn, Shadeequah, Blessing, Demond, Rayshawn, Justin, Jovan, Daquai, Everton, Kevin Michael, Kiara, Diamond, and all of your children—this book belongs to all of you.

To Bee Phox, my cousin and co-visionary—thank you for walking with me through music, life, and the grind.
Your spirit and creativity helped me dream again.

To the brothers and sisters I met through struggle, especially those behind the walls—you are not forgotten. To Kilpatric Mitchell, Abdul Malik Shabazz.

You are seen, and your stories matter.

To everyone who doubted me—thank you. You pushed me harder than you'll ever know.

To those who believed in me when I couldn't believe in myself— thank you from the deepest part of my soul.

To Lisa Ascolese, The Inventress—your faith in Reyena gave my vision wings.
To Gearhart Law, and all the professionals who helped turn my invention into reality—I'm grateful for your commitment.

To Governor Phil Murphy, thank you for granting my pardon. Your act of justice gave me peace, dignity, and a new start.

To my Pardon and Expungement Attorney, H. Robert Tillman—thank you for standing beside me with skill, honor, and heart. Your work changed my life.

To John Harmon—thank you for your powerful letter to the Governor. Your words helped open the door to my freedom.

To every reader—thank you for taking the time to walk this road with me. I hope my story inspires you to rise again, no matter how far you fall.

Don't block your blessings.
And don't let the past define your future.

With love and respect,
Hugh Carter

PROLOGUE: FROM ASHES TO REDEMPTION

Some people talk about rock bottom like it's a moment.
For me, it was a fire.

I was a young man when I jumped from that burning house. Flames behind me. Family inside. My baby nephew **Shawn Darnell Carter** didn't make it out. He was just three years old. And with him, a part of my youth went up in smoke.

We lost everything that day.
The roof over our heads.
The photographs that held our history.
Even the air we breathed changed forever.

But that was just the beginning.

I've survived through conflicts and survived battles in the streets of Trenton. I've worn a uniform and a DOC number. I've stood in front of judges and in front of microphones. I've seen the inside of a cell and the inside of my soul. And through it all, one thing kept calling me: **redemption**.

Not just freedom—but *transformation*. Not just survival—but *purpose*.

This book isn't just about what I went through. It's about what I *became* because of it.
It's about the lessons fire couldn't burn and prison couldn't erase.
It's about finding light after the darkest hours, and building something out of brokenness.

I've been labeled a felon, a fighter, a hustler, a survivor.
But I also became a veteran, a businessman, a mentor, an inventor— and a man who earned a full pardon.

Not because I begged for it.
Because I changed.

This is not a book of excuses.
It's a testament to what's possible when a man takes ownership of his past and dares to rewrite his future.

This is the story of how I lost everything, found myself, and walked back into the world with nothing to hide and everything to give.

I ain't goin to jail.
Pardon me? I've already been redeemed.

CHAPTER ONE:
THE JUMP, THE LOSS,
AND THE FAMILY LEFT
BEHIND

It was during the end of 1980 at 58 Kelsey Avenue, Trenton, New Jersey. My mom Alice Harris headed out to work as a cook by bus to PJ''s Pancake House on Nassau Street in Princeton, NJ directly across the street from The Ivy League's Princeton University like always.

My sister Wetonah Carter sent her sons Reginald and Demond off to school then she went to the laundry mat . Our house—small, wood-framed, and filled with life—went up in flames so fast we barely had time to breathe.

The house was filled with smoke when I was awaken to horrifying screams from my Uncle's wife Rose below "The house is on fire!". I was 18 years old when our house caught fire — a moment that scorched its way into my memory forever.

🔥 The Fire

The fire broke out fast, and we were trapped inside. I tried to run downstairs but the smoke and fire pushed me back into the room. As I re-entered the room.

I thought is this the way my life is about to end! All I could see was clouds of thick smoke.

The smoke filled the hallways and began to start filling my lungs. I can feel the intense heat rapidly increasing as I re-entered the room, panic overtaking logic, and saw my cousin Charles Phox escaping through the second-story window. I followed him without hesitation.

I jumped—arm burning, hair singed, lungs full of smoke. I remember hitting the ground. I remember the chaos.

I remember the fireman Robert Ervin pulling my brother Kevin and nephew Aaron from the roof. I remember the sirens, the screaming. And I remember the cold silence when we realized not everyone had made it out.

Aaron was only two years old and was in such guarded condition that he was airlifted to the Children's Hospital of Philadelphia Acute Care Unit. Miraculously he survived.

I was taken in an ambulance with my three-year-old nephew Shawn Darnell Carter who fireman Blaine Shaddo found under a bed while they fought the fire for about 40 minutes.

I remember looking at him, thinking he was asleep — but he had already passed away from smoke inhalation, they pronounced him dead at 10:30am that morning. \

It had taken more than 20 firemen from five city companies to fight the blaze at 9:05am that morning. That moment has never left me.

That fire took more than just a house. It took our peace. It took Shawn. And it burned something deep into me — a survival instinct, a need to fight through life's flames no matter how hot they got. It was chaos and heartbreak wrapped into one.

That article serves as a permanent reminder of what we endured. Standing outside the charred house, grief frozen on their faces. Aunt Estelle took us in after that. She was my second mother. Her kindness and structure helped us survive.

💔 Loss of Shawn Darnell Carter

What's truly remarkable—what still amazes me to this day—is that out of the tragedy of losing my three-year-old nephew, Shawn Darnell Carter, came the miracle of new life. At the time of the fire, my sister Wetonah was pregnant.

She was doing what any young mother does—caring for her children, trying to hold it all together. While she was away, everything changed.The fire took **Shawn**. There's a photo I still

have—miraculously recovered from the remains of that fire.

I look at that photo sometimes and wonder how something so fragile as an image could endure such heat—when a life so young could not.

This was during the **Christmas Holiday** season as you can see in this image with his brother Aaron in the background.

I had taken this picture and it survived the fire somehow with a few other things like albums and a melted 45 record that I still have today!

However just a few months later, My sister gave birth to another son. She named him **Rayshawn**—a name that carried Shawn's memory like a torch.

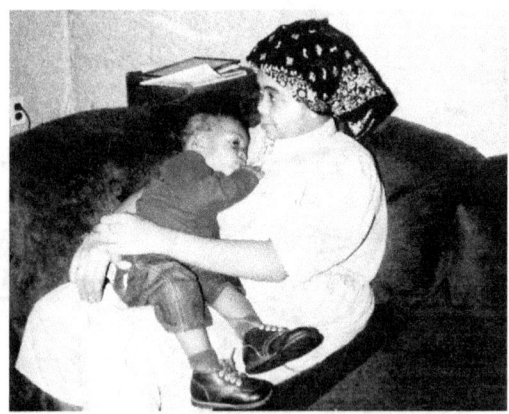

It was her way of honoring what she had lost while holding tight to what remained. That name symbolized strength, resilience, and the will to keep moving forward, even in the face of heartbreak.

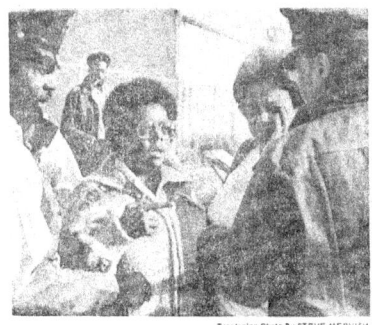

Boys Played With Matches Often Before Fatal Fire

By CHUCK DAVIS
Staff Writer

An early morning rowhouse fire that killed a 3-year-old Trenton boy and left his 2-year-old brother in guarded condition yesterday was apparently started by one of the children playing with matches, according to a fire official.

The blaze which ripped through the 2½-story frame home at Kelsey and Short Avenue in the West Ward, "appeared to have been started when a match was dropped into a stuffed chair in the middle room of the first floor," said Battalion Chief Joeseph Stein.

Neighbors and relatives told the chief one of the children had a habit of playing with matches, Stein said.

Shawn Carter, 3, was pulled from the second floor of the burning building by fireman Blaine Shaddo, but life-saving efforts at the scene and in the hospital failed to revive him, officials said.

He was pronounced dead at 10:30 a.m. in Mercer Medical Center.

His brother, Aaron, 2, pulled from the flames by fireman Robert Ervin and rushed to Philadelphia's Children's Hospital by helicopter, was listed in guarded condition in an acute care unit, a hospital spokeswoman said.

Six other persons were in the home when the fire began, Stein said. There were taken to the hospital and treated and released.

The children's mother, Wetonah, was at a nearby laundromat when the fire began, officials said.

Rosie Nollie, 20, visiting the Carter's with her two children, Nicki and Reinell, spotted the fire and escaped to the roof of the home. The two Carter children apparently did not follow Nollie, officials said.

More than 20 firemen from five city companies responded to the blaze at 9:05 a.m. and fought it for 40 minutes Stein said.

The fire spread to the adjoining building, occupied by Mary Allen, but was stopped before it burned through the roof, Stein added.

The persons treated and released were identified as Thomas Carter, 18, Charles Harris, 20, Charles Phox, 20.

TRAGIC FIRE — Wetonah Carter, mother of three-year-old Shawn who was killed in a fire early yesterday in their home in the West Ward, speaks with Trenton Police Sgt. Vander McFarland and a fire official when she learned of the fire. A neighbor looks on.

Trentonian Photo By STEVE MERVISH

But what still bothers me is how the tragedy was misreported in the local media. The Trentonian newspaper ran a story that completely distorted the facts. According to the article, children were playing with matches at 9:00 a.m., and a 20-year-old adult named was wide awake, supposedly in the house. It was written as if the entire thing was the result of negligence or reckless behavior.

My late mother, **Alice Carter-Harris**, was not mentioned by name in the newspaper article documenting the fire.

They clearly didn't identify my mother **Alice Jean Harris** whose is pictured with my Aunt **Estelle Phox** who had came down from Princeton where my mother was at work and had gotten the message and made it back to the house. They identified my mother as my sister!

I never believed that version of the story. I still don't.

They couldn't even get the basics right. They spelled my name wrong, and they spelled my brother Kevin's name wrong too. They listed our ages incorrectly—Kevin was 17 and I was 18 at the time. Worse than that, the article completely left out one of the most critical parts of what happened that day.

They never mentioned that my cousin **Charles Phox** and I jumped from the second-story window to escape the fire. We were forced to leap through the smoke and flames, not knowing if we would land safely or survive. That jump was pure instinct —survival in its rawest form.

And they also failed to mention how the **Trenton Fire Department** rescued my brother **Kevin** from the roof of the house.

That's the truth. Not exactly the way it was printed.

What happened that day was devastating, but what followed was also a story of survival—of a family torn apart, but not completely broken. The world only saw the fire. What they didn't see was everything we went through in the smoke, the chaos, and the aftermath. And they certainly didn't see the courage it took just to keep going.

Let me give you a deeper sense of my family during that time. My mother had five brothers: **Ernest 'Uncle Juney' Johnson Sr.**, **Jesse Carter** was already deceased, **David Carter**, and the **twins James and Jerome**.

My father, **Hugh Lovejoy Harris**, had passed away the year before the fire. He had one brother, **Joe**, and eight sisters: **Grace, Estelle, Louise, Lucy, Margaret, Pauline, Sylvia**, and **Frances** who perished in a home fire in her youth.

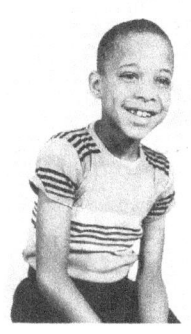

I never had any children of my own, but I've always carried the weight of family as if they were all mine.

And though I would go on to live many lives—soldier, prisoner, businessman, inventor—this was where it all began. With fire. With loss. With family.

My mother's father, my grandfather, **Arthur "Little Joe" Coles**, was from **North Philadelphia** and was an **Army veteran**.

He traveled by train to Trenton regularly, and as I later learned, he was also a bookie. His brother was **Little Johnny Coles,** he'd made a name for himself as a famous jazz musician from Philadelphia.

No memoir would be complete without acknowledging the profound influence of my mother, **Alice Jean Carter-Harris.** she possessed a heart of gold, always willing to extend a helping hand and share whatever she had with others. Her

kindness and generosity were evident in her actions, particularly in her role as a cook and server at **PJ's Pancake House**.

Mom devoted herself to providing nourishment and care to those who visited the establishment, leaving an indelible mark on the community. My mother, Alice Jean Harris also worked as a waitress at the **Nassau Inn**. Both within walking distance from **Princeton University on Nassau Street.**

Mom had a zest for life that found expression in her love for two particular activities—bingo and dancing. These were sources of joy and excitement for her, allowing her to unwind and immerse herself in moments of fun and camaraderie.

Whether it was the thrill of marking off numbers on a bingo card or the sheer delight of moving to the rhythm on the dance floor, Mom embraced these activities with enthusiasm, leaving lasting impressions on those who had the pleasure of joining her.

My mom caught the bus to work and sometimes taxi cabs. She didn't drive. I loved when she brought us extras from work with dessert. Everyone ate at PJ's. They enjoyed my mom's cooking. All of the cops, prosecutors, doctors, nurses, students, faculty and lawyers went there.

A lot of my family and friends worked there including myself as a busboy. Everyone called her Mom such a sweet lady who would give you her last, she had five brothers. More about them later.

My father came into a city rich in history but also in turmoil. South Trenton was where they settled. My Mom and Dad later married after I was born. We lived on Clay Street in Trenton.

Right around the corner from my grandmother **Alice Mae Carter** house on Market Street. Right down the street from the **Mercer County Detention Center**.

My dad separated from us and moved to Princeton. He worked as a carpenter and later on at **Carter Wallace** in West Windsor, NJ.

We later moved to **Passaic Street**. **The West Side**. Later known as **God's Ave. Peace to Da God's!**

My mom loved bingo and dancing. We had a few bars around the corner called the **Desert Inn**, **The Horseshoe** and **Klotz.**

There also was a Liquor store on the corner next to my friend's Church. My dad was an avid hunter and fisherman. Often eating what he caught with his friends. He never took us fishing. He was a former Army veteran and member of the Rod and Gun Club of Princeton.

More than likely washing it down with those empty liquor bottles that me and my brother would see on his dresser. Whenever we'd go see him, he would give us allowance. Five dollars was good back then! My dad was off that Thunderbird and my mom drank Miller.

My dad's, father and mother was **Rosa and Joseph Harris** from **Charlottesville Va**. I didn't get to meet them. More about them later on. My dad's brother, Uncle **Joseph Harris** served 24 years in the Army he went to Korea and Vietnam getting hit with Agent Orange.

My Uncle Joe was hilarious. He would tell us all kinds of stories about his time in Vietnam. He would send us to the liquor store called Tash in Princeton as soon as they opened up for a fifth of vodka.

Trenton was once the **Capital** of the **United States**, a battleground of the Revolutionary War where the Hessians were defeated. Trenton, New Jersey is comparable in size to Compton, California. In close proximity to New York and Philadelphia.

But by the time I was born, a different kind of war was unfolding—riots, political unrest, and the lasting impact of the Vietnam War on families like mine.

Kevin was left-handed, I was right-handed, and from the moment he could hold a ball, he was my competition. He could shoot the lights out when we got older, and whether it was basketball or anything else, he always pushed me to be better.

As a child, I witnessed my mother and father fight, their relationship unraveling before my eyes. Eventually, they separated, and we moved from South Trenton to West Trenton.

Life was different on the other side of town. Some of the boys my age and I fought each other at first, testing boundaries, but in time, we became friends.

My sister, though—she was tough. If someone messed with me, she'd hurt them, no hesitation, no second thoughts. Despite the family struggles, childhood had its moments of joy. We played games like cops and robbers, 1-2-3 red light, house, and hide and seek.

My crew formed a little clique called the Daredevils. We'd dare each other to do the wildest things—jump on the back of a moving ice cream truck, hop onto a moving train. We we're about 7 and 8 years old or so, with our friends.

Looking back, we had no fear, just the thrill of the moment. Growing up, family was everything. My Aunt **Martha** and Uncle **Earnest Johnson**—who we all called "Uncle Juney"—had nine children: six boys and three girls. That's him bottom right corner in this historical Army photo.

Most of them were older than me, and they lived just around the corner, up the hill. It was like having extra big brothers and sisters. We had a ball every time we got together, like a daily family reunion.

Their house had its own unique character.

They always kept half a pig in one of their refrigerators, and the pungent aroma of hog mogs or chitterlings would hit you as soon as you walked up to the house. But the best part was the energy in that home.

We used to call the boys "The Johnson Five plus One"—
Earnest Jr., Moses, Frank, Michael, Eugene, and Jamey, better

known as "Smokie." Vivian, Kim and Jennifer filled out the
roster. They would play music and sing, filling the house with
rhythm, laughter, and life. Those were the kinds of moments that
made childhood unforgettable.

My cousin "Smokie" was also a lifeguard at the Trenton
YMCA, thought it was funny to playfully try to drown me one
time. I didn't think it was so funny, but that was the way we grew
up—playing rough, testing limits.

I had a friend named Howard. Every morning before
school, he'd rob his dad of pocket change, climb out the window,
and we'd take our money—along with the dollar my mother gave
me—and buy as much candy and cookies as we could before
school started.

That was our social media, lol! Just running around, getting into things, making memories. Life changed when my mother met a man named Ronald Greene—who I would later call "Pops." He had kids of his own, and just like that, our family expanded.

Mr. Greene had the gift of gab, the type of man who could talk to anyone and get things done. They called him the Mayor of Passaic Street. He had connections, real ones—with City Hall and Trenton's actual mayor, Arthur Holland.

Mr. Greene was a great man who would later become my guardian angel! Every summer, he made sure the neighborhood kids had block parties and free bus trips to the shore.

He even turned on the fire hydrants in the summer to cool us down. But tragedy came early. Mr. Greene's oldest son, Ronald Jr. "Ronnie", died on my birthday in a horrific accident on the Southard Street Bridge in Trenton when I was just 10 years old.

We didn't wear seatbelts during that time. His loss hit hard—he had been a great addition to our extended family. Mr. Greene's other son, Reginald and brother William and sister Jaqueline, became part of my world, but Ronald's death was one of the first times I felt real grief.

Discipline in our household was no joke. We got beatings —belts, extension cords, switches—whoever had permission to lay hands on us did.

Step Pop, babysitters, Mom, Uncles, even my Grandma Alice Mae who was known for sending you out in the yard and peeling your own whooping which was a switch if you acted up. She was sweet though would give us nickels or dimes to go to the store and buy cookies and candy for ourselves.

One day she made a special meal when things got tough. My Uncles James and Jerome was twins, they came home late one day. They had a pet rabbit named Chee - Chee.

They came in the house late for dinner. After finishing their meal, my Uncle Jerome says to his Mother Alice Mae, my grandmother.

"Where's Chee - Chee". He loved that rabbit. My grandmother was from **South Carolina** said to him. "You ate her!" My sister started laughing. My Uncle Jerome was the heavier twin! Times was tough that week. It was just how it was back then—if you messed up, you paid for it, no questions asked. Maybe if they would of came home sooner. He said the rabbit was good though with the meal. When I recently asked him about what my sister had told me! She was there! That's the only picture that I have of Grandma Alice Mae with her one of her five sons, my Uncle David.

Still, through all of it, I was a happy-go-lucky kid who knew how to hustle. If I wanted something, I had to find a way to earn it. I shoveled snow in the winters, sold a newspaper called GRIT. I sold the Trenton Times.

I sold Amway it was soap powder at the time and helped people carry their groceries to their car.

I often took the neighborhood school bus provided by the city to go work on a farm picking fruit or vegetables early in the morning when the sun came up until the afternoon. Then you weigh everything on a scale for a few dollars a day.

Hard work didn't scare me—it was just part of life. But it wasn't all work. We played outside every single day until the streetlights came on. I would finish my homework at school. So I could stay outside because I didn't want the kids that I hung out with to see where I lived.

You had to be from my neighborhood. We made zip guns out of wood, nails, rubber bands, and clothespins, using soda can tops as ammunition. It was all in fun—just boys being boys, testing limits.

My brother Kevin and I loved music and we had a band in the neighborhood with our own club the street. In a garage called **Disco 3000.** We was right around the corner from the group **Instant Funk** a famous group from Trenton.

I became a Boy Scout, part of an all-black Troop. "**Troop 105**, don't take no jive", that was our cadence when we made the newspaper as young Boy Scouts for marching from **Trenton Statehouse** to **The Morven in Princeton**. That was where I learned discipline and survival skills.

Meanwhile, the world around me seemed to be in chaos. Assassinations were common—Malcolm X, Martin Luther King Jr., John F. Kennedy and Robert Kennedy. It felt like every time we turned around, another leader was gone. But as kids, we lived in our own world, finding joy in the little things.

My cousin **"Smokie"** taught me how to skate at the Capital Roller Rink in Trenton, where skill and style mattered. He was amazing on wheels, he could do anything flips, speed and twist and go backwards really fast. He was so good he became a member of the Philadelphia Roller Derby League.

The Capital Roller Rink became a significant gathering place for me and my friends. Skating alongside my cousin "Smokie," who was regarded as the best skater in town. I honed my skills and formed connections.

It was there that I even met **DJ Ready Red** before he joined the **world-famous Geto Boys.**

Trenton had the **Mayfair Theatre,** where we'd go to escape into the world of movies. **The Mack, Cotton Comes To Harlem, Enter The Dragon** and **The Exorcist.** Some of the all time classics!

I collected DC and Marvel comics from the bookstore downtown for five cents a piece, fascinated by the superheroes who seemed to always find a way to win, no matter how bad things got.

And sports—sports were everything. We played whatever we could, wherever we could. Basketball, baseball and football. I'm front row center number 20.

The neighborhood kids and I were always looking to get together, always finding ways to compete, laugh, and make the best of what we had.

Trenton was a city of potential, but it was also a city of struggle. It was an industrial powerhouse, but not everyone prospered. The Vietnam War changed families, taking fathers and brothers away, and some never came back the same.

But through it all, I was just a kid trying to navigate my way, learning the lessons—some hard, some easy—that would shape the rest of my life. I didn't know then how much this city would mold me. I didn't know how many battles I'd have to fight—both in the military and the streets.streets and within myself. But I knew one thing for sure: I was a survivor. And that was just the beginning.

CHAPTER TWO:

RECESS OF MY LIFE

· ·

After the fire, all I had were the memories in my mind.

No baby pictures. No family photo albums. No comic books or action figures. No Sunday suits or hand-me-down jeans.

The fire didn't just burn the house—it erased my childhood. Everything tangible, everything you'd normally hold on to, was gone. What was left were echoes—moments buried deep in the corners of my memory.

So I closed my eyes and went inward.

I began to walk through the recess of my life. Not recess like the playground, but the hidden spaces—the forgotten rooms in the back of my mind where joy and pain sit side by side. Where I could still hear my mother humming in the kitchen. Where I could feel the warmth of my father's voice, even though he had already passed. Where I could see little Shawn running around barefoot, laughing, just days before the fire took him.

Grief has a way of sharpening memories. Sometimes I remembered more than I wanted to. Other times, I struggled to remember anything at all. But it was all I had. My past was no longer a photograph on the wall. It became a story I carried in my heart, frame by frame, breath by breath.

I didn't understand it at the time, but surviving that fire was the beginning of a lifelong search—not just for purpose, but for identity. For truth. For the pieces of myself I thought I lost in those flames.

I was just a boy, standing in the ashes, trying to make sense of what came before. And somehow, I knew this was only the start.

Trenton, New Jersey, my hometown, is steeped in American history. It played a pivotal role during the Revolutionary War, with the Battle of Trenton marking a major turning point in the fight for independence. Just days later, the Battle of Princeton added to the city's legacy, etching it into the nation's story as a site of defiance and resilience.

Growing up there, I was surrounded by reminders of this past.

The Old Barracks Museum stood as a living monument just downtown, preserving the **Revolutionary War** history that was literally in our backyard. The Delaware River flowed not far from my home, with the Morrisville, Pennsylvania Bridge crossing over it—just around the corner. We were down the highway from the **Sparkling Champale Company**, and practically neighbors with the old **Magic Marker** factory. You could smell the ink in the air when the wind blew just right.

Trenton wasn't just a historical landmark—it was an industrial powerhouse. It thrived on manufacturing: auto parts, trucking, rubber, glass, plastics, and electrical components.

It was a working city, a gritty city, where people hustled to feed their families and hold on to a piece of the American dream.

Tomato pie—our own twist on pizza—was a local staple, and **Prince Whipple**, a Black Revolutionary War hero who crossed the Delaware with Washington, remains one of the city's unsung legends.

Even the shaky pedestrian bridge over Route 29, near where the **Trenton Thunder** baseball team now plays at the stadium beside the Cure Insurance Arena, had its own place in the city's character. Every creak and sway felt like a metaphor for the city itself—weathered, enduring, and still standing.

In 1968, when the Trenton Riots broke out following the assassination of Dr. Martin Luther King Jr., I was just six years old. But I remember the tension in the air. The anger. The fear. The fire. The National Guard rolling through the streets of a city that had suddenly become a war zone in its own right. That moment left a mark on me—on all of us. It was the first time I witnessed how deep the wounds of injustice could run, and how quickly a city that had helped birth a nation could erupt in pain.

Trenton wasn't just where I lived—it was part of who I was. A city of history, hustle, heartbreak, and hope.

School was always an adjustment for me and my siblings. We moved around a lot, which meant switching schools often. We started at Parker School in South Trenton, then went to Grant School in East Trenton, followed by Monument School in North Trenton. By the time I got to Cadwalder School, I had already figured out that no matter where I went, school came with rules —and consequences.

Teachers back then didn't hesitate to discipline you. I learned that the hard way, standing in front of the class with my hands outstretched as a ruler cracked down on my them.

The sting was sharp, but so was the lesson—act right, or face the consequences. That kind of discipline didn't just happen at home; it was everywhere. My sister, Wetonah, went to Catholic school, where the nuns didn't play either. She got her share of discipline too.

After grade school, my sister, my brother Kevin, and I all ended up at Junior High School #3 in West Trenton—our last stop before high school. It was here that Kevin and I had one of the craziest realizations of our lives. We used to joke about this kid we saw in the hallways—a dude with an afro just like ours, same color, same shape. Every time we saw him, we'd nudge each other and say, "There go your brother." Then the other would shoot back, "Nah, that's your brother!" It was just a joke —until one day, we found out it wasn't.

Turns out, he actually was our half-brother Craig from my dad side. I had on a white tuxedo on my Junior Prom Night. My brother Kevin in the middle of our images. Craig is on the right, my older brother, whose an artist. His mother Bonnie confirmed that Craig is my brother.

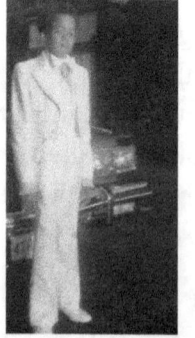

I would also find out later on from my dad side of the family that we are related to **President Thomas Jefferson.** We are gate keepers at Monticello in Charlottesville, Virginia. **The Daily Progress in Virginia** did an article with my first cousin **Paul C. Harris** about our familial ties.

Life had a way of throwing surprises like that, but in a place like Trenton, you learned to just roll with it.

While attending Junior High School #3, I had my eye on this girl named Evette. I kept trying to get a chance with her, but no matter what I did, I always failed. Someone else had her interest already. She came from a family of fighters—real fighters.

Her father was legendary. It was told to me by former Professional boxer Army Veteran, turned correction officer and **International Professional Boxing Referee** Lindsey Page one day at the **Veterans Affair Medical Clinic** that Evette's father hit so hard that one day he punched a cow in the head at a Correctional Facility and knocked it out. His was a legendary puncher. More later on.

All of his sons were fighters too, and three of them even became professional boxers: Very talented and gifted brothers, definitely nothing to play with. But me? I wasn't interested in the brothers—I wanted to talk to their sister! I really did like her, but that family? They were always boxing or fighting. It was just in their blood.

While I was unknowingly discovering new family members in school, my mother's oldest brother, **Earnest Johnson Sr.**, was building his own legacy. He was a tough man —a boxer and an Army veteran who moved from South Carolina with his mother to Trenton my grandmother, **Alice Mae Carter.**

His son Moses told me that whenever Uncle Juney boxed **Ike** at **Trenton Pal** that he'd beat Ike, boxing was in his blood, and he made a name for himself by beating a well-known lightweight boxer from Trenton.

I remember Uncle Juney would come pick us up in his car, and I'd be in the backseat, frustrated because at four or five years old, I was too small to see over it. He would drive us to New York to visit family, drunk as can be, sometimes even swerving onto the sidewalk.

Yet, somehow, he never got pulled over or into an accident. Uncle Juney and Aunt Martha his wife were related to **Smoking Joe Frazier** by marriage he attended Aunt Martha's funeral here in Trenton, NJ. He drove himself and mingled with us!

My Uncle James was a master painter—he could paint an entire house by hand in just one day. In fact, he became a historical painter back then. He also worked as a driver for a former **Trenton Mayor,** alongside the mayor's chief of staff, Bill.

The mayor lived on the same block as Uncle James, and he used that driving job to build a network of private clients who would pay him to drive them wherever they needed to go. Which was also down the street from the former mayor of **New York.**

Strength ran in the family, whether it was inside the ring or out in the world. As I got older, I eventually learned how to swim, and on hot summer days, we would head to the community pool known as the **Bubble.**

It was within walking distance, and every kid in the neighborhood would be there, splashing around, cooling off, and showing off their best dives. Those summers were simple and carefree, filled with laughter and the relief of cold water against the heat.

Downtown Trenton had its own appeal too. We had a **McDonald's,** where cheeseburgers were just 15 cents—a small price for a big treat. This was during the time when pork was king in Trenton.

Case Pork Roll and **Taylor Pork Roll** were local staples, two original Trenton products that had people arguing over which one was better. And then there was **DeVito's Pizza** downtown—a slice from there was always worth the trip. We had **Snyder's** were you could buy seven dollar Chuck Taylor Converse Sneakers everyday or walk further downtown to **Woolworth** and cop some **BoBo's** for two dollars!

Family cookouts were a tradition, bouncing back and forth between my mother's small house on Passaic Street and my Uncle Earnest Johnson Sr.'s house. Those gatherings were some of the best times—plenty of food, laughter, and music. But cookouts in my family weren't always just about good times.

When my Uncle David came home from prison—after serving time for killing a man—he stayed with us for a while. He killed the guy who killed his brother Jesse, after being threatened by him, I never got to meet Uncle Jesse. Uncle Dave didn't eat pork and went out of his way to show us why.

But as kids, we weren't trying to hear it—pork was cheap, easy, and everywhere. Still, his conviction made me think, and I started paying attention to the choices people made and the reasons behind them.

The more I learned about my family, the more I realized how much history—both good and bad—was shaping my life. When I learned how to play cards we eventually started playing for nickels, dimes and quarters.

Sometimes we would play all night laughing and joking. We would play a game called spades. This one guy knew how to cheat real good until we caught him one day. His name was Wesley.

Cookouts weren't just about food and family bonding. Once the wine and beer started flowing, things could take a turn. My Uncle James and his twin brother Jerome, along with Uncle David, would start telling stories—sometimes arguing, sometimes throwing fists. They could really fight too, and when things got heated, it wasn't just words being thrown—sometimes it was weapons.

That was just the kind of family I came from—fighters. In my neighborhood, it wasn't just my uncles who knew how to throw hands.

We had plenty of professional boxers and street fighters, men who had built reputations with their fists. Growing up around them, I learned quickly that respect wasn't given, it was earned—and sometimes, it had to be taken.

Those summers, those cookouts, those lessons—they all shaped me. I was just a kid, but I was already starting to understand that life wasn't just about having fun or getting by. On my mom's side, family was everything back then.

We were tight, even though the occasional fight would break out. The cookouts were some of the best times—music blasting, laughter filling the air, and dirt kicking up in the backyard where the grass had long since worn away.

My mom was only five feet tall, while my dad stood at six foot one. But my biological father never took us anywhere. That weighed on me, especially in school when kids would come back from summer vacation talking about all the fun they had with both their parents. I never had those stories to tell.

No kid ever says they want to grow up to be an alcoholic, a drug addict, or a dealer. But addiction can start off small, almost innocent—maybe gambling, playing cards for nickels and dimes. Staying up all night playing cards can shape a person's mindset, feeding into habits that spiral over time.

Despite it all, I once told my guidance counselor in junior high that I wanted to be a lawyer. It was about survival. And in Trenton, you had to be ready for whatever came your way. But no kind of strength could prepare me for how quickly I had to grow up.

My sister Wetonah got pregnant when she was just thirteen years old, making me an uncle at twelve. My brother Kevin was eleven. That changed everything.

She gave birth to a boy named **Reginald**, and you wouldn't have even known she was pregnant—she carried it like nothing had changed. But everything had.

At twelve, I was still a kid myself, but I had to learn quickly how to be an uncle. Then, the next year, when I turned thirteen, she had another son, **Demond**. Looking back, maybe that's where my hustle really started—watching my sister take on the responsibilities of being a mother while still being a kid herself.

By the time I turned fifteen, she had her third son, **Shawn**. At this point, we were moving from place to place—a different house, a new neighborhood, a new situation. We would also spend time at **Cadwalder Park**, a place where families gathered for cookouts or just to relax on a nice summer day.

It was one of those spots where you could breathe, where the worries of the neighborhood felt a little further away, even if just for a few hours.

Family history ran deep in our lives, and the lessons of survival were passed down through generations. Uncle Jessie and Uncle Earnest had taught their younger brothers how to fight, making sure they could hold their own.

However being known for your hands wasn't always a good thing. Uncle Jessie was jumped by five guys with lead pipes—they knew how well he could fight, and jealousy played a role, too. He had a lot of girlfriends, and that made him a target.

In Trenton, being good at something—whether it was fighting, making money, or getting attention—could make people love you or hate you. Sometimes both.

By 1976, my life started to shift in other ways. That year, I met a young lady from another neighborhood in my class at Junior High School Number #3. She stood out to me immediately. I started carrying her books and walking her home every day. It was a small gesture, but for me, it meant a lot.

I was in 9th grade, still a little shy, and dealing with the realities of my living conditions. Compared to some of the kids in West Trenton, I felt poor, and that insecurity made me hesitant. But this girl? She was beautiful, and she carried herself like a young woman. Meanwhile, I still looked like a little boy in my eyes.

Despite my doubts, something about her made me step out of my comfort zone. We ended up going to the Junior Prom together. I was already an uncle by then, watching my sister raise her kids, but deep down, I still just wanted to have fun.

That moment—dancing at the prom, standing beside her —felt like a glimpse of something bigger. Maybe, just maybe, there was more waiting for me outside of everything I had known.

Stability wasn't guaranteed, and I started realizing that life wasn't waiting for me to catch up. I had to keep moving with it!

I remembered what it felt like walking into Junior High School as a shy, skinny teenager with the biggest Afro in the class. I wasn't the loudest, but the girls noticed me—mostly because they loved braiding my hair after school. I didn't say much, but I didn't have to. That Afro did enough talking for both of us.

Even though I was small for my age, I loved sports like I was built for it. I was proud to be on the track team and the football team. I remember the rush of winning, the joy of winning that championship trophy with my teammates. I earned a certificate in both sports, and that meant the world to me. For once, I felt seen—not just as the quiet kid with the big hair, but as someone who could win.

But things started to change by the time I got to Trenton High School.

"Sometimes the streets teach you faster than a textbook. But the lessons come with a cost."— Hugh Carter

When I first got to Trenton High School, I was still an honor roll student. I walked in with my head held high, carrying the same drive and discipline that had gotten me that far. But it didn't take long for things to change.

I had a lot of friends by then, and like most teens, I was eager to grow up fast. I'd gotten my driving permit, which felt like a badge of independence. The only problem? I didn't have a car. So I'd catch the bus to school like everybody else—at least at first.

It wasn't long before school took a backseat to other interests. My friend and I started skipping class, creeping out of the building to go hang with our girlfriends. That's when the drinking started too. One of my boys had a car, and the deal was: I could drive it—if I drank a can of Old English Charcoal Brewed Beer. I was 17. Didn't take much peer pressure at that age to say yes.

That's him and his Grand Prix. you can also see Korvette's Department Store in the background behind the tire shop late 1970"s.

That was the era when I had more than a few girlfriends. I was young, feeling myself, and thought I had it all figured out. But I was slipping. Grades fell. Focus faded. I wasn't just hanging in the hallways—I was shooting dice in them. I'd be mid-roll on the floor, and the second we heard the principal coming, we'd scatter—bolting down the corridor like it was a track meet.

Looking back, I can see I was on a different kind of path. The wrong one. But at the time, it felt normal—just part of growing up in Trenton, where temptation waited around every corner, and reputation often mattered more than report cards.

Somewhere along the way, I began to pick up bad habits. I started drifting from that kid who made the honor roll to someone the teachers started giving up on. The streets started looking more appealing than the classroom. And before I knew it, I was a high school dropout.

Not because I wasn't smart—but because I was searching for something school couldn't give me at the time: identity, control, power, even respect.

Still, something inside me wouldn't let me fall completely.

I would later get my G.E.D., and enroll at Mercer County Community College in Trenton. Eventually, I made a decision that would change the course of my life: I enlisted in the United States Army.

I didn't know it yet, but the boy who dropped out would soon be running with an M16 on his back serving this Country. That shy teen with the giant Afro? He was about to become a soldier. But first, there was still more of the world—and myself —I had to face.

At 18, I was legally an adult, and my sister was 19. By then, she had her fourth son, Aaron. I had seen her grow from a teenage girl into a full-time mother, and it made me more protective of her.

I loved my mom, my sister, and my brother, and I understood that family wasn't just about being related—it was about stepping up when it counted.

With all the moving, all the changes, and all the responsibilities stacking up, one thing was clear: childhood was over. It was time to grow up.

Soon I would start training on my own. Running up and down the bike path on route 29 in Trenton. Doing calisthenics. Then me and a friend Walter Polk started working out together and eventually Lamar " Raheem" Hicks would run through our neighborhood in West Trenton to the Leprechaun Gym in South Trenton and that's where I met Cedric "Special K" Green and Lyndsey " Monster" Page who wanted to spar with my friend Walter who was bigger than Lyndsey but wasn't ready! However, Walter would parlay the workouts into a 100lb weight loss and sparring with Jesse Boston. While I was preparing for my mission!!

CHAPTER THREE:

TRENTON TAUGHT ME

. . . .

The streets of Trenton were rough—always were. But for a young Black boy trying to make sense of life after loss, they were also a classroom. And every corner, every cracked sidewalk, every set of stairs we sat on, became part of the curriculum.

Trenton taught me how to watch. How to listen. How to move.It taught me that not everything that looks dangerous is—

and not everything that smiles at you is safe.

After the fire, we moved from place to place, trying to find stability in a city where most people were just trying to survive. Aunt Estelle took us in, gave us a roof and a little bit of peace. But life didn't slow down to give us time to heal. It kept moving—and if you didn't keep up, you got left behind.

Trenton wasn't just a city—it was a proving ground.

In the late '60s and '70s, the city was buzzing with a dangerous rhythm. You could hear it in the arguments across porches, and see it in the eyes of kids barely old enough to shave, already carrying the weight of men. I was one of those kids.

After the fire, after losing my father, and trying to adjust under the care of Aunt Estelle Phox, I found myself drifting between the rules of home and the raw code of the streets. I had to learn fast who to trust and how to move. Trenton didn't allow for hesitation. Either you learned to protect yourself or you got swallowed.

I wasn't a bad kid—but I was angry. I was hurting. And in Trenton, that often meant being recruited by the streets before you knew what was happening. You started by running errands. Then you held something. Then you did something. Before long, you were part of it, whether you meant to be or not.

But the streets weren't just about crime. They were about survival. Camaraderie. Loyalty in its own twisted form. Some of the realest lessons I learned about trust and betrayal came from those corners. I had friends who turned on me. I had enemies who saved my life. Trenton taught me to read people faster than books ever could.

And yet, I knew I couldn't stay on that path forever. I had dreams—even if I didn't know what they were yet. I didn't want to become another headline, another "what happened to Hugh?" story. There was something in me, even then, whispering that I was meant for more. It would take time, pain, and a whole lot of detours—but I never forgot that whisper.

I remember the older guys on the block. Some had jobs, some hustled, some didn't do much of anything at all. But they all had an edge. An awareness. They were alert, always scanning. Even back then, I was studying them—trying to understand what made a man respected, what made him feared, and what made him invisible.

School was its own battlefield. Not just the classrooms, but the unspoken rules in the hallways, the tension in the lunchroom, the pressure to prove yourself without losing yourself. Some of us made it through with our heads down. Others got swept up in the wrong crew, the wrong decision, the wrong moment.

But Trenton wasn't just pain—it was people. Real people. I saw resilience in the mothers who worked two jobs and still made dinner every night. I saw joy in the neighborhood cookouts, the music blasting out of basement windows, the kids playing tag until the streetlights came on.

And I learned that there was a difference between being alive and actually living.

Most folks around me were just trying to do both.

It was in Trenton that I first realized:

you don't have to go looking for trouble—if you're poor and Black in America, it'll find you.

But Trenton also taught me how to stand in the storm and not flinch.

This city raised me. It scarred me. But it gave me my fight.

After the fire I found out that my father had left me an inheritance. I wasn't expecting that. However he did name me after him. I paid for a lease for a five bedroom home and fully furnished it for my family.

I didn't know my father, Hugh Lovejoy Harris, was an Army veteran until after he passed away. He and my mother had separated when I was still a kid, and like so many children raised in divided homes, there were entire chapters of his life I never got to read until the book was already closed.

But here's what I eventually learned: my father served in Korea, just like his brother Joe Harris. Two brothers, both in uniform, both fighting in a way that many have forgotten, but which shaped a generation of strong, quiet, working Black men. Learning that truth filled me with a quiet pride—a deeper respect for the man whose shadow I had unknowingly walked in for years.

I remember one thing he told me when I was a teenager. He looked at me and said, "Cut those braids out your head and join the Army."

At the time, I laughed it off. I was young and rebellious. I liked my braids. The girls liked them too. Structure and uniforms weren't part of my plans. But what I didn't realize then was that those words were a seed. He saw something in me before I could see it in myself. And when I eventually did join the Army, that seed had already begun to grow.

After serving his country, my father became a carpenter down in Virginia. He worked with his hands—measuring, cutting, and building structures meant to last. It wasn't just a job. It was a skill. A discipline. And years later, without planning it, my baby brother Kevin became a carpenter too. He picked up the same tools and carried on the tradition—creating something from nothing, just like our father.

And me? I may have taken a different road, but I still found myself later on working with my hands. At one point in my life, I was building gas furnaces for The Trane Corporation—precision work, real work, the kind that requires both focus and pride. Just like my father. Just like Kevin.

It's funny how life connects us in ways we don't even notice at the time. Military service. Carpentry. Manufacturing. Generations of men in my family didn't just work—we built. We crafted. We created with our hands and served with our hearts.

We carried more than our last name. We carried a legacy of service, skill, and strength.

However right now it was party time. I took care of my mom, brother and sister with the inheritance and then we had a great time in our newly furnished home also my brother and I rented an apartment in Philadelphia at the same time.

Before I joined the Army, my brother and I had already begun tapping into the pulse of a cultural revolution. In 1982, we launched **Rose Royce Entertainment**, name after the luxury automobile. Our mission was to bring the emerging energy of hip hop to life through parties, performances, and community events —and we were doing just that.

We didn't just keep it local. While we were based in Trenton, we threw parties in Philadelphia and even branched out to the Norristown area, reaching into new scenes and expanding our influence. These weren't just small gatherings—some of them drew large crowds of young people hungry for this new sound. We booked local talent, and even had well-known acts like **Kurtis Blow** perform at our events. Kurtis was already a hip hop pioneer at that time, known for songs like **"The Breaks"** and **"Basketball."** The fact that we had him involved showed we were playing in serious circles—even if we didn't fully grasp the opportunity in front of us.

Looking back now, had we known how to properly run and scale a company, Rose Royce Entertainment could have become something historic. We had the vision, the access, and the timing—but not the business structure, capital, or mentorship.

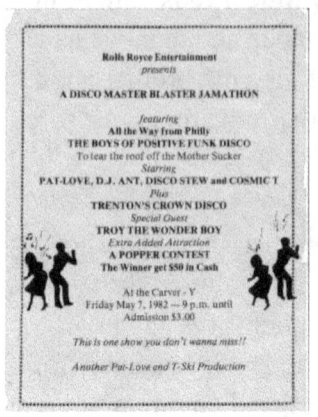

Promoters who stuck with it—like Russell Simmons, who co-founded Def Jam in 1984—were able to turn their party-hosting hustle into multimillion-dollar legacies. We didn't know it then, but we were right on the edge of something big.

If We Knew Then What We Know Now...

Even in 1982–1983, hip hop events were pulling crowds of 300–500 people, sometimes more. At $5–$10 per head, that meant $1,500 to $5,000 in revenue per night. Running 2–3 shows a month, we could've earned between $30,000–$60,000 a year— which in today's money (adjusted for inflation) is the equivalent of $90,000 to $180,000 annually. That doesn't even include potential income from concessions, artist booking fees, or merchandise.

Had we kept pushing—expanded further into Philly, Camden, Newark, or the New York boroughs—things could've looked very different. If we'd branded ourselves, managed talent, and distributed mixtapes, Rose Royce Entertainment might've been the first major hip hop imprint from Trenton. We could've been Trenton's answer to Def Jam, Bad Boy, or Roc-A-Fella.

Even though the company only lasted about a year two, from 1982 to 1984, those moments taught me the basics of hustle, organization, and opportunity. It planted a seed. That early experience helped shape every future chapter—whether managing artists under 2Souljiers, promoting boxing matches, or eventually inventing Reyena. It was a preview of the entrepreneur I'd later become.

We had brought **Kurtis Blow** to Trenton and hosted parties at the **Carver Y in Trenton. Parties in Philadephia and Norristown**. Until the money ran out!

That's when I said forget that **"I Ain't Goin To Jail"**. Some of the people I had been hanging with had robbed a liquor store and shot the guy and got caught. That's when I walked downtown Trenton into the Army Recruiting Station and signed up!

I partied everyday the week before I went in. I served during the Lebanese Crisis and Operation Urgent Fury in Grenada.I didn't even know that then!

The Army taught me how to serve

By the time I joined the military, I wasn't just looking for a way out—I was looking for something solid. Something that couldn't burn down, disappear, or turn its back on me. The United States Army became that thing. I enlisted with the weight of loss on my shoulders and the streets of Trenton in my bloodstream.

Basic training wasn't easy, but I wasn't new to hardship. I knew how to follow orders. I knew how to stay alert. I knew how to move as a unit because in the hood, we had to move as one or get picked off one by one.

What surprised me was how natural the military felt to me. The structure, the mission, the brotherhood—it all gave me a sense of purpose I hadn't felt in a long time.

The streets taught me how to survive. The Army taught me how to live.

I enlisted young. It wasn't just about patriotism—it was about escape. I needed distance from the chaos, from the traps of the neighborhood, from the weight of loss and struggle. I needed something bigger than me. And I found it in the U.S. Army Infantry.

Basic training stripped me down. No more attitude. No more ego. Just sweat, discipline, and grit. But I adapted quickly. The structure, the unity—it gave me purpose. I started to feel like I was part of something that mattered.

Then came the real test.

I served during the Lebanon Crisis and Operation Urgent Fury in Grenada. Real missions. Real consequences. Real blood. You don't come back the same man you were when you left. And the truth is, some part of me never came back.

We wore the uniform with pride, but we still had to fight for respect—sometimes from our own ranks. Being Black in the military was like being Black anywhere else in America: you had to work twice as hard to be seen as half as good. Still, I gave it everything I had. I showed up. I did my job.

When I was honorably discharged, I didn't even realize I was a Disabled American Veteran. I just knew I was coming back home to a world that had changed—and I had changed too. I thought serving would be enough to earn peace. Instead, I returned to find chaos had just been waiting for me to come back.

But before all that—before the struggle, before the street temptations started calling again—I was a soldier. I stood with boots in the dirt and duty in my heart.

And for a moment, that felt like enough. While sustaining injuries during service I began self medicating to cope with the pain that I was in everyday. Not a good idea, I would find out later.

When I came home from the Army in the mid-1980s, the country I had served was battling a new kind of war — a war in the streets.

Crack cocaine had flooded communities, especially Black neighborhoods like mine in Trenton, New Jersey. It wasn't just a drug — it was a system of destruction.

You survive conflict, but can you survive coming home?

There's no parade waiting for you when you get off that plane. No band, no banners. Just regular people doing regular things — while you're standing there changed in ways you can't explain.

Coming home from the military ain't like the movies. I stepped off that base with an honorable discharge and the kind of silence that speaks louder than any gunfire I heard.

I wasn't just tired. I was fractured.

I came home looking for stability, but what I found was chaos. The streets were full of temptation, fast money, and faster consequences. Despite my military discipline, I got caught up in that environment.

The reality is, the transition from soldier to civilian was not as simple as just switching uniforms. I didn't have a guide. I didn't even know I had benefits. All I knew was I had to survive.

When I came home from the Army, I wasn't the same kid who left. But the world I returned to wasn't the same either. It was the early 1980s, and the crack cocaine epidemic was spreading across the country like wildfire—and Trenton, New Jersey, was no exception.

Jobs were scarce. Opportunities even scarcer. The pressure to provide, to survive, to stay afloat was relentless. I didn't come back to a hero's welcome. I came back to a battlefield in the streets. And this time, the enemy looked like my own neighbors, friends—even family.

At first, I tried to keep my head down. I worked jobs where I could. But when you're a young Black man with no college degree and no real guidance for dealing with the trauma of military service, you start to lose direction. The wrong people offer quick money. And when you're broke, broken, and angry… you listen.

I came home from the Army expecting something.

Respect. Stability. Opportunity. Maybe even peace.

But what I came home to was… nothing.

No parades. No job offers. No resources. No guidance. Just silence.

I had served my country, stood tall in uniform, followed every order, and did everything right. But when the dust settled and the boots came off, I realized America didn't owe me a damn thing—and it had no problem reminding me of that. I was just another Black man back in the system. Back on the block. Back to square one.

Nobody ever told me I was a disabled veteran. I didn't even know to ask. I didn't understand what I was owed, what I had earned, or how to navigate the paperwork and politics of veterans' benefits. And to be honest, even if someone had handed me a checklist, my pride might've made me ball it up and throw it away.

So I did what I knew—I hustled.

I picked up jobs here and there. I kept my head low, tried to stay out of trouble. But it wasn't long before the streets started calling. Old faces. Old temptations. The fast life was always around the corner. It offered quick money, fake love, and a place to belong—even if that place came with handcuffs and court dates.

The crack epidemic was exploding. It was like a tidal wave hitting every city, every block, every family. And it didn't care if you wore a uniform or a prison jumpsuit—it came for all of us.

Coming home wasn't the relief I thought it would be. It was a test. One I didn't know I was taking. And I was failing it.

Not because I was weak—but because I was tired.

Tired of fighting battles with no weapons.

Tired of being strong with no support.

Tired of surviving when I just wanted to live.

But that's the thing about being from Trenton. About surviving a fire. About being a soldier. Even when you're tired—you don't quit.

The 1980s hit Trenton like a hammer. The streets that once echoed with music, block parties, and neighborhood legends began to pulse with something darker.

Crack cocaine. It didn't just show up—it exploded. Fast money, fast deaths, and faster downfalls. I saw it unravel my city block by block, person by person.

I tried to stay clean. I really did. But when doors keep closing on you—when the job applications lead nowhere, when you're overlooked, when you're still battling unseen trauma from the military—it becomes too easy to make one bad decision. Then another. Then you're in.

I got caught up. And not just a little.

A4/THE TIMES, WEDNESDAY, SEPTEMBER 30, 1987

Seven arrested in drug raid at Ewing apartment

By JACK KNARR
Staff Writer

TRENTON — Seven people were arrested yesterday in a Ewing Township drug raid at a Parkside Avenue apartment complex.

The raid, at the Parkside Court Apartments, was conducted by municipal and county officials following a two-month investigation, officials said.

Mercer County Prosecutor Pete Koenig charged two of seven suspects as 'kingpins' under New Jersey's tough new drug law that could put them in prison for life if they are convicted.

Charged as leaders of the alleged crack cocaine manufacturing and distribution ring were Samuel Taylor, 20, of the 1600 block Parkside Ave., Ewing, and Kevin Harris, 24, of the 100 block Cleveland Ave., Trenton.

They were charged with drug trafficking, maintaining a controlled dangerous substance production facility and distributing drugs within 1,000 feet of a school.

Mercer County Special Services School for mentally and physically handicapped children is located within 1,000 feet of the apartment, Koenig said.

Koenig estimated that the ring did about $50,000 worth of business a week.

Seven Ewing Township Police officers and four members of Koenig's Special Investigations Unit (SIU) combined in the raid on the apartment leased by Harris in the complex at Parkside Avenue and Buttonwood Drive. The raid followed a two-month investigation, said SIU Lt. Al Heyssey.

Arrested on the same charges and held overnight without bail at the Mercer County Detention Center for arraignment this morning were four Trenton men: Robert E. Highsmith, 20, of the 100 block Passaic St.; Charles Black, 23, of the first block Kelsey Ave.; Walter A. Polk, 26, of the first block Passaic Ave., and Hugh L. Carter, 25, of the 100 block Cleveland Ave.

A 17-year-old boy was also arrested and charged with possession and distribution of cocaine and possession with intent to distribute.

The evidence included 11 ounces of loose crack worth $22,000, 2,430 packaged vials of crack worth $24,350 at $10 a vial, $4,994 in cash found on the living room floor and four ounces of marijuana worth $640.

Crack is a smokeable form of cocaine.

Police also confiscated a police scanner, three pistols — including a .357 Magnum — and a shotgun, and narcotics paraphernalia used in the

cooking and packaging of crack. Also confiscated were two automobiles, a Volvo and Mercedes, both 1979 or 1980 models.

Staff photo by Marc Bellagamba
Mercer County Prosecutor Pete Koenig displays some of the drugs and money seized during a raid at a Ewing apartment complex.

I was swept up in what would become the largest drug raid in Mercer County history at the time. They came hard and heavy—battering rams and boots on the ground. I'll never forget the sound of doors being kicked in before the sun came up. It felt like war all over again, only this time the battlefield was my own backyard.

This wasn't just about me. My youngest brother, Kevin Harris, was caught in the storm too. He and another co-defendant were charged under the newly established drug kingpin law instituted in April 1987, a tough New Jersey statute aimed at dismantling drug networks. They were labeled drug kingpins—a title that carried a heavy, nearly impossible burden to beat. They were facing life in prison.

As for me? I was charged with possession and possession with intent to distribute. They tried to tie me in by proximity. We were brothers—so they painted us with the same brush. They wanted to bury us.

The courtroom wasn't about justice. It felt like a game already decided before we walked in. We were young, Black, and from Trenton. In their eyes, that was enough. They didn't care about my military service. They didn't care about the trauma I brought home. They saw a statistic.

But I wasn't just a statistic. I was still fighting to live. Still fighting to prove that I was more than a mistake.

Eventually, I got caught up in the process. I made mistakes. Bad ones. Ones that cost me everything.

Survival instinct I learned in the fire and in the military kicked in — but this time, it was the wrong battlefield. I made decisions that led me down the wrong path, and eventually, I got arrested.

I Didn't Know I Was Disabled

Let me say that again, because it took me over two decades to say it with clarity:

I was a Disabled American Veteran — and didn't know it.

I left the Infantry with pain in my body and noise in my head, but no one told me I qualified for help. No one handed me a brochure. I wasn't briefed on what to watch for, who to talk to, or how to heal. And I didn't ask — because soldiers don't ask.

That's how I carried invisible wounds for 24 years.

Pain that got chalked up to "just life." Anxiety that I swallowed and ignored. A back that didn't bend like it used to. A heart that didn't trust peace.

But I didn't complain. I was just glad to be alive — until I realized being alive and being well were two different things.

The Crack Era Had Arrived

While back in Trenton, it didn't feel like home. It felt like a war zone of a different kind. One where the bullets came in glass vials and the soldiers were just kids trying to make it through the day.

The crack epidemic was full-blown. Families were getting eaten alive. And the traps were everywhere — in the streets, in the laws, in the looks people gave you when they knew you just came home.

It was easy to fall into the rhythm of survival. You blink and you're in something you swore you'd never be part of.

The same skills that kept me alive during conflict — awareness, toughness, calculation — weren't enough to save me from the streets. You could get caught slipping. And eventually, I did.

They say when you fall, it's fast. But mine was slow — decisions stacked on decisions. A hustle here. A mistake there. A circle of people who didn't see the future I saw.

And the next thing I knew, I was in court. Then in chains.

Then in a cell.

I was arrested, tried, and sentenced to seven years in state prison. Just like that—no more freedom. No more control. Just concrete walls and steel bars.

You don't have to be free to start changing.

You just have to make the decision to stop dying slow.

That moment in prison—sick, weak, halfway gone—changed me. Not just physically, but spiritually. I stopped asking, Why me? and started asking, What now?

I still had years ahead of me. Cold nights. Countless roll calls. Faces I didn't trust. Traps I had to dodge. But I made a decision: If I couldn't walk out of prison a free man yet, I would at least walk out a better man.

So I started rebuilding.

I read. A lot. Anything I could get my hands on—law, business, psychology, autobiographies. Malcolm. Mandela. Military history. I went to war with my own ignorance. Every book was a brick. Every thought I wrote down was a blueprint. I was building something—even if I didn't know what it would become.

I also started listening more. Not to the noise, not to the gossip—but to the men who had wisdom. Some had been down for decades. Some were never getting out. But the ones who had evolved, the ones who still had light in their eyes, taught me things I never learned in school or in the streets.

And for the first time in a long time, I looked in the mirror and didn't hate who I saw.

I didn't just want to get out—I wanted to walk out with something no cell could ever hold:a vision.

I thought about my past—the fire, the Army, Trenton, my family—and I started writing it all down. The pain. The survival. The hustle. The fall. I wanted to leave a trail, so maybe somebody else wouldn't have to fall as hard.

Because it hit me: I wasn't just a felon. I wasn't just a number. I wasn't just what the world saw.

I was still me.

And I still had something to give.

I didn't wake up one morning and decide to be a criminal.

It was never about wanting to break the law—it was about trying to bend life into something that made sense. Trying to survive.

The streets don't wait for anyone. They're always open. Always hiring.

And when you come home from the military with no job, no support, and no clear path—you start answering to whatever calls your name. For me, it was the hustle.

At first, it was just about making ends meet. A little something here, a little flip there. I told myself it was temporary. I told myself I had it under control.

But the truth is, the hustle doesn't come with brakes. Once you're in, it starts to drive you. You don't even realize you're being driven off a cliff until it's too late.

The crack era didn't just change the streets—it transformed them into war zones. Everyone was armed. Everyone was desperate. And the line between predator and prey got thinner by the day. You weren't just hustling product—you were hustling your soul.

I saw friends get rich fast and disappear faster. I saw families fall apart. I saw funerals become more frequent than birthdays. And I saw myself slipping further from the man my mother raised. The boy who had survived the fire. The soldier who had worn the uniform with pride.

But once you're in deep, pride can't pull you out.

I started moving differently. Paranoia became normal. Trust was rare. The same streets that once taught me how to watch my back were now teaching me how to guard my heart. Because betrayal came easy. Loyalty didn't.

It all caught up to me. The deals, the dirt, the danger. One day, I found myself facing a sentence I never imagined—and all I could think was: How did I get here?

But deep down, I already knew.

The hustle didn't just take my freedom.

It took the version of me that still believed I could be something more.

After my brother Kevin and I were arrested, it sent

shockwaves through our family. But no one was hit harder than our mother. She took it very hard—so hard, in fact, that she suffered a mental breakdown. That moment broke something in her, and though she tried to stay strong, she never fully recovered.

I carried the weight of that every single day.

I was ashamed of how far I had fallen—ashamed that my addictions and the choices I made had not only ruined my own life, but had deeply hurt the one woman who had always stood by me. I had spiraled out of control, and that spiral dragged my mother down with it.

But I wasn't beyond saving. I sought help—and found it through the Veterans Administration. They extended their hand at a time when I didn't think anyone would. Through their programs, I was able to receive the kind of counseling, treatment, and rehabilitation I needed to get back on my feet. They helped restore not just my life, but my sense of purpose.

Most importantly, they gave me the tools to start making things right with my mother. I knew I could never undo the pain I caused, but I could be there for her. And I wasn't alone. My sister Wetonah was a rock during that time. She and her children stepped in and helped care for our mother—taking her to appointments, making sure she was safe, and giving her the love and support she needed when her world was crumbling.

"Turning Toward the Light"

There's a moment when you realize you're still alive for a reason. Not just breathing—but alive.

That moment hit me when I walked out of the VA hospital with a treatment plan and the first piece of hope I'd held in years.

When I finally went to rehab, I came face-to-face with a truth I had been avoiding for years: I was using alcohol to self-medicate the pain I carried deep inside. I thought I was managing it—numbing the hurt, coping with the memories—but what I was really doing was fueling an addiction just as destructive as any street drug. I learned quickly that alcohol isn't just socially acceptable—it's dangerously deceptive. It can hook you in and drag you down just like heroin, crack, or pills.

What's more, I discovered that alcohol can be a gateway —not just to harder drugs, but to a whole world of destructive behaviors. Gambling. Reckless sex. Anything that offered an escape. Addictions don't discriminate—they creep into every corner of your life. And more often than not, I'd come out the other side financially broke, emotionally drained, and spiritually empty. I wasn't living—I was surviving on fumes, throwing my life away one drink, one bet, one bad decision at a time.

That chaos, that insanity, was over 33 years ago now, thank God. It took humility, surrender, and a whole lot of help to break the cycle. I had to accept that I was powerless over the addiction. And believe me, that wasn't easy.

But admitting that powerlessness was the first step toward true strength and clarity. I wasn't in control—addiction was.

Part of my recovery wasn't just about getting clean—it was about making things right. I made my amends to the community I had harmed in ways both seen and unseen. I looked people in the eye and owned up to my mistakes. That was a heavy burden, but it lifted something from my soul. I wasn't the same man anymore, and I didn't want to be. I was ready to build —not destroy.

I found a better way to make my own path. A path rooted in purpose, in healing, in truth. I stopped hustling backwards and started moving forward with intention. I realized I could still be somebody. I could still make a difference—not despite my past, but because of it.

To anyone out there struggling: get help. Don't wait until you've lost everything. The pain you're drowning in won't go away with another drink—it'll only grow louder. Recovery gave me my life back. It gave me a future. And I promise you, it can do the same for you.

I was far from healed, but I was finally pointed in the right direction. The Veterans Administration didn't just treat me like another case file—they treated me like a man.

A man who had served his country, made mistakes, and still had value. They didn't judge me for the prison time, the addiction, or the pain I carried. They met me where I was and showed me how to rebuild from the ashes.

In those early days, I had to face myself. Not just the things I'd done, but the man I had become—and the man I still wanted to be. I had to look in the mirror and confront the years I lost, the family I hurt, and the pain I caused my mother. I couldn't change the past, but I could fight for the future.

I started with small steps. Attending every appointment. Staying clean. Making the calls I'd been too ashamed to make. My sister Wetonah answered with love, not judgment. Her voice alone gave me strength. And her children—they welcomed me back into their lives like no time had passed. That kind of grace is rare. I didn't take it for granted.

My mother was still fragile, still hurting. Kevin's life sentence weighed on her every day. But even through her sadness, when she looked at me, I could see something I hadn't seen in a long time—hope. She saw her son trying. And that meant everything.

I remember sitting next to her during one of her medical appointments, holding her hand. She leaned over and said, "I see you trying, baby. Just don't stop." That was the fuel I needed. Her strength, even broken, was stronger than most people's at full force. I owed it to her—and to myself—not to stop.

Recovery wasn't a straight line. There were moments I wanted to give up. Days when the weight of my past felt like it would crush me. But I kept showing up. I kept praying. I kept healing.

I started reading more. Writing. Thinking. I began imagining a life where I could use my experiences—not to bring shame—but to bring change. I wanted to give my story a purpose. Maybe if I could come back from everything I'd been through, someone else could too.

And that's where the idea of redemption really began to take shape in my heart. Not just as a wish, but as a mission.

Still, the weight my mother carried about Kevin was too heavy. My baby brother had been sentenced to life in prison. That devastated her. No mother should have to carry the pain of losing one son to the streets and another to the system. Her heart was broken in a way that even time couldn't heal.

Seeing her like that changed me. It lit a fire in me to never go back—to fight for my healing and to do better not just for myself, but for the people who had never given up on me. My mother, my sister Wetonah, her children—they were the reason I pushed forward.

People think prison is the punishment. It's not. The punishment is everything that comes after. It's the scarlet letter they brand on your name—"convicted felon." It follows you to every job interview, every lease application, every hopeful new beginning.

But even in prison, I made a vow: This will not be the end of my story.

I kept my head up. I educated myself. I stayed out of trouble. I planned for something better. Because I knew deep down that I wasn't a criminal—I was a soldier who got lost coming home.The streets taught me how to survive.

That scarlet letter — "convicted felon" — followed me like a shadow. It wasn't just time behind bars. It was a mark that would make everything harder for years to come.

But even in that dark place, I never gave up. I told myself daily, "I ain't goin to jail again." I refused to let my story end in a cell.

That's what they gave me.

Seven years for a man who once fought for this country.

No matter what my uniform had said before, now the only label that mattered was: Convicted Felon.

"I left the Army with no mission. So the streets gave me one. And it nearly cost me everything."

CHAPTER FOUR:

HUSTLE, HEART AND

HOSPITAL BED

....

While I'm beginning to walk out of those prison gates, I was free—but I was not the same man who walked in. I wasn't bitter. I wasn't broken. I was determined.

But freedom doesn't come with a map. No welcome home committee. No job waiting. Just the label of a felon, a fresh pair of sneakers, and a mountain of stigma stacked against me.

You don't just get out of prison — you fight your way back into life.

As I'm stepping out of that prison gate, the sun was hitting different. It was warm, but it didn't feel welcoming. I wasn't free — not really. I was on paper. On watch. On edge.

And I was still wearing the scarlet letter: convicted felon.

You think you're going to walk out and start fresh. But the world doesn't hand you fresh starts. You have to carve them out with blood, sweat, and dignity. No one cared that I had served this country. No one cared that I had served my time. All they saw was a number, not a name.

Now that I'm all of the way out of those open gates, the air felt different.

Not because I was free, but because I was different.

I hadn't just done time—I'd done work. On myself. On my mind. On my mission.

But freedom wasn't easy.

Coming home after prison is like walking into a world that moved on without you. You're expected to pick up where you left off—but the truth is, everything's changed. People. Streets. Opportunities. And most of all, you.

I came back with a new energy. A hunger for something real. No more half-living. No more shortcuts. I was done with fast money and fake loyalty. I wanted to build something that couldn't be taken away with one mistake.

So I got to work.

I took jobs nobody else wanted. Day jobs, night jobs. Warehouse, security, retail—didn't matter. I was clocking in when others were clocking out. Not because I loved the grind, but because I needed the discipline. The structure. The steady ground. And I needed to prove to myself that I could stand on my own two feet without leaning on the streets.

There were moments I wanted to quit. When old temptations whispered in my ear. When I saw people getting money the fast way. But I reminded myself: I already paid that price. I already wore that number. I already danced with death— and I walked away.

This time, I was choosing life.

I stayed around my family. I leaned into my faith. I started dreaming again. Not wild dreams—but focused ones. Purpose-driven. I wanted to use my story to build something bigger than me.

And even though it wasn't clear yet what that something was, I could feel it forming.

Right there beneath the surface.

Still, I never gave up.

I got engaged to Donna Guinyard, a good woman who stood by me when I needed something steady. But life doesn't always reward you for doing right.

One night, I made a mistake—a drunken street fight. I was arrested for improper behavior, a charge that stemmed from a brawl that never should've happened.

While in lock up at the Police Department, I started feeling sharp pain in my left knee. **Something wasn't right.**

While in the Police Department Jail for being observed street fighting improper behavior at initially I was denied medical attention for my injuries and out of the blue my stepfather Ronald Greene Sr. had heard my cries for help, he worked at the jail doing janitorial work, Thank God! I was in excruciating pain he said son what are you doing in here! I told him I got arrested for fighting and I'm hurting the **blue shirts** won't help me they keep walking away.

I showed him my leg. So he said hold on and went and got the **white shirt** otherwise I would have died that early morning like so many others during that time.

I can't tell this story without mentioning **Ronald Greene** —my **stepfather**, who worked at the **Trenton Lockup**.

Somehow, someway, he found out I was in danger.

He pulled every string he had.

Made the call.

Got the word to the right people.

And just like that, the guards who had been ignoring me **changed their tone**.

I got proper treatment.

I got attention.

I got saved.

Ronald wasn't just a father figure.

In that moment, he was an **angel in uniform.**

He passed years later, but I still say this with all my heart:

He was my guardian. And I owe him my life.

I was transferred from jail to the hospital for what was supposed to be a one-week recovery.

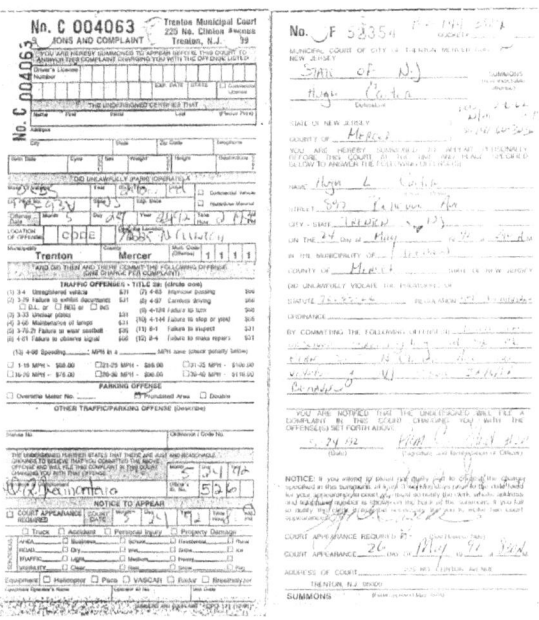

It was on May 24th, 1992, at approximately 2:40 a.m., I was arrested and ticketed by the **Police Department.** The summons said I had been observed "street fighting" at the corner of Grant and North Clinton Avenue, a violation the Statute under Improper Behavior.

But the truth was far more complex, and painful— literally and figuratively.

That night I was outside of a fast food restaurant—not inside, as some would later try to claim. I was never in the establishment. I was outside the entire time. According to the discharge summary from the Medical Center, I was described as a 30-year-old Black male who, while allegedly inebriated, "fell down and injured both knees." It stated I was in police custody for about 12 hours before being brought to the ER because of "complaints of pain in both knees and an inability to stand on my left leg."

The hospital's version of events didn't match the reality at all. I didn't fall. I was jumped on. I had eyewitnesses who saw plainclothes officers slam me to the ground and kick me in the head and step on me that morning.

But from the moment I read the medical report, I knew something wasn't right. The report said I fell exiting the restaurant—again, I never entered. That detail alone made me feel like the they may have been in on the fix too. It all seemed like an orchestrated cover-up.

And what made it worse was that I wasn't some out-of-shape guy stumbling around the streets. I was a veteran. I took pride in keeping myself physically fit. Even after my honorable discharge, I maintained a disciplined routine.

I used to run up to five miles a day. I was in shape—strong, alert, and still holding onto that military mindset. So when the doctors told me after the surgery that I'd never run again—at just 30 years old—it hit me hard. Real hard. It felt like they didn't just rupture my knee—they ruptured a piece of my identity. That's not something you get over easily.

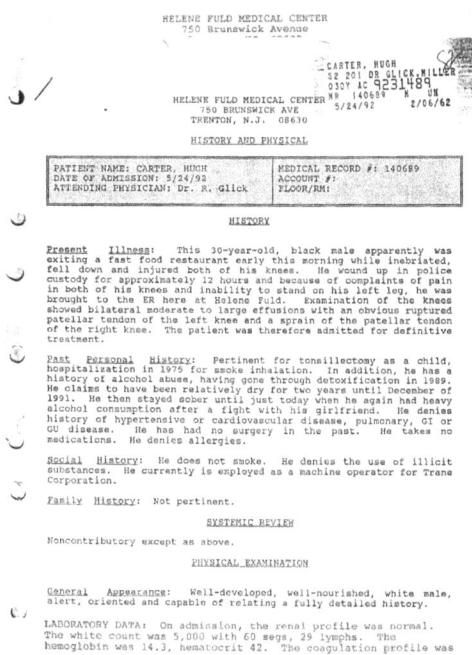

What happened next was a nightmare. I was admitted to
Helene Fuld soon in critical condition. The diagnosis: ruptured
medial patellar tendon in my left knee, a sprained patellar tendon
in the right, and—most frightening of all—an acute pulmonary
embolism that nearly took my life while I was in therapy.

They said when I woke up that I was pale as Michael
Jackson. they described me as a well developed, well nourished,
white male in their report.

I was placed in bilateral knee immobilizers, underwent
surgery on my left knee, and spent days recovering. I was on IV
medication, underwent blood tests, scans, and had a syncopal
episode that nearly turned fatal. Afterward, I had to learn how to
walk again using a walker, then crutches.

I was discharged on June 13, 1992, in "improved condition," but nothing felt improved. I was still furious, traumatized, and determined to get justice.

The Slow Recovery and Spiritual Awakening

Healing was slow. I didn't bounce back.

But I did *wake up*.

Lying in that hospital bed, surrounded by the sound of machines and the weight of reflection, I had to ask myself:

- What are you going to do if you get another chance?

- What will all this pain mean if you don't turn it into purpose?

- How many more lives do you get before God says, "Enough"?

It wasn't a dramatic, born-again, fall-to-my-knees conversion.

It was a quiet, slow, intentional decision to **change**.

Not just my behavior.

My mindset.

Time Served, But Not Wasted

I did my time.

I walked that yard.

I held my head high.

And when I was finally released, I didn't just come home
—I came back **different**.

Smarter.

Sharper.

Stronger.

I had survived the courts.

Survived the cells.

Survived my own body trying to take me out.

And now?

Now I was on a mission.

Months later August 21, 1992, after I had recovered enough, I filed a lawsuit against the Neighborhood Police Department. I hired an attorney from the town, hoping he'd fight for me like I needed. But looking back, he did me no favors. In fact, he hurt my case more than he helped it.

From the beginning, I could tell he didn't do his due diligence. His initial letter had the wrong date of the incident May 23, 1992. He clearly hadn't even read my medical report. The most basic facts were wrong, saying that I had ruptured ligaments in my left knee. Minimizing what actually happened. He was negligent.

By January 1994—just before the statute of limitations would run out—he notified me that he no longer handled those types of claims. Just like that. No fight. No warning. Nothing. I felt betrayed again. It was a gut punch.

I never got my day in court. It's spilled milk now, and I've made peace with it over time. But I write this not just for the record—but as a warning.

Watch who you hire to represent you. Not everyone in a suit is there to defend your rights. Some are just there for the check. And some, like that attorney, will walk away right before the finish line, leaving you to pick up the pieces.

A blood clot formed after surgery and traveled through my body. It caused my left lung to collapse, and I was rushed into the Intensive Care Unit (ICU) at Helene Fuld Hospital in Trenton—barely clinging to life. My blood pressure was 60/40 pulse of 90.

```
1  ..a the right knee, and 60 ccs. of bloody fluid without fat
1  .ng obtained from the left knee.  Patient was then placed
1  .teral knee immobilizers.  On 05/25/92 the patient was ta
t  .he Operating Room, where under general endotracheal
a  .sthesia, surgery to the left knee was performed.  The
l  .perative diagnosis was that of a ruptured patellar tendc
t  . operative findings being a complete rupture of the media
r  .inaculum, the remainder of the knee being normal.  Theref
t  . patient underwent exploration of the joint, and repair c
r  .al retinacula.  He tolerated the procedure well,
l  .peratively being started on intravenous Ancef and is bei
c  .inued for 48 hours postoperatively.  He was maintained i
l  .teral knee immobilizers for the first 24 hours.  On the
s  .ond postoperative day, he was placed into a CPM machine.
l  .a low grade temperature for the first three hospital day
t  .i became afebrile.  On the third postoperative day he was
t  .hysical Therapy, where gait training was intiated, with
t  ..r, full weightbearing as tolerated, and the patient bei
l  .ained in the knee immobilizers.  On the fourth postoper
c  .is dressings were changed, and the wound to the left kn
t  .lean and dry.  By the sixth postoperative day the patie
t  ..bulating in Physical Therapy with a four point gait wi
c  .hes, but he was having difficulty with stairs.  On the
s  ..th postoperative day while in Physical Therapy the pati
l  . syncopal episode, followed by difficulty breathing, an
c  ..oresis.  His blood pressure was 60/40, pulse of 90.  An
i  .venous was started and the patient responded to hydrati
c  .eing placed in the supine position.  An EKG at this tim
i  .ively normal as noted above.  A ventilation perfusion s
c  ..e lung was performed, and as noted above, was felt to s
l  . suspicion for pulmonary embolism.  Consequently, Medica
```

From a drunken mistake to fighting for my next breath.

And through it all, by my side, was Donna—my fiancée at the time. She didn't walk away. She nursed me back to health. She washed me, fed me, stayed through the pain, and prayed when I couldn't speak. That kind of love doesn't come around often. And I'll never forget it.

I survived. Again. And this time, I woke up with a new mission.

After everything—the prison, the pain, the street fight, and the ICU—I knew my life had to mean something. I wasn't just getting up for myself anymore. I was getting up for a purpose.

I didn't wait for a job to fall in my lap — I went after whatever I could find. Two jobs. Sometimes three. Anything to keep me moving forward. Anything to make sure I never had to look back.

I worked when I was tired. I worked when I was hurting. I worked when people laughed at me or looked past me.

After I married Donna, I began working at the Trane Corporation. It was a solid union job—came with full benefits and plenty of overtime opportunities. I was grateful for the steady income and security, but I never stopped aiming higher.

I was married then. I had responsibilities. Rent don't care about your past. Bills don't care about your pain. And love — love needs to be fed with action, not just intention.

Driven by a desire for a better future, I enrolled in computer school while still working full-time. Every day after my shift, I would head to The Chubb Institute Keystone School in Springfield, Pennsylvania in 1995, where I studied Computer Technical Support. It wasn't easy juggling both responsibilities, but I was determined. That hard work paid off when I graduated with a 4.0 grade point average.

I had hoped this new path would open doors to a better career. But after graduation, I discovered the harsh truth: entry-level tech support didn't pay as well as my warehouse job.

Despite the diploma and the long hours I'd put in, I made the tough choice to stay where the money was.

In the end, I remained at the warehouse for nearly seven years—holding it down while quietly keeping my dreams alive.

I used to hustle to survive.

Now, I hustle to build.

When I got back on my feet, I wasn't just chasing jobs—I was chasing legacy. I had learned the hard way that real power doesn't come from what you can flip in a week—it comes from what you can build to last for a lifetime.

I started diving into business. Not just working jobs, but studying the system. Learning how money moves. How companies scale. How leadership works. I didn't want to be a pawn in someone else's game—I wanted to create my own board.

That's when I found **Excel Communications.** It wasn't just a job—it was a classroom. I worked my way up. Trained teams. Spoke on stages. Learned to lead.

And for the first time, people listened to me not because they had to—but because I had something real to say.

That experience rewired me.

It showed me that I had skills the streets couldn't take away:

Discipline. Drive. Charisma. Vision.

It showed me that I wasn't just a former inmate—I was an entrepreneur in the making.

It was my brother in law, Darryl Guinyard, who introduced me to **Excel Communications**—a company that would help change the course of my life.

Excel offered a chance to work from home as an Independent Representative, selling long-distance service and building a team. You could earn bonus checks and residual income. And most importantly, you didn't have to lie about your past to get in.

"Don't just make a living—make a life worth living."

The Excel Era: From Ground Floor to Regional Director

Then came **Excel Communications.** They were offering something I'd never heard before:

Work from home. **Residual income.** A chance to own your time.

It sounded too good to be true. But I was hungry. And I was ready to hustle.

I signed up as an **Independent Representative** and started learning the game. Sales. Cold calls. Home meetings. I wasn't just selling phone services — I was selling belief. And I believed hard enough to pull others in.

I climbed the ranks — Independent Representative, **Area Coordinator, Senior Director.** Then:

Regional Training Director and **Regional Director.**

I was in rooms with the top earners. I met the owner, **Kenny Troutt,** himself — a billionaire. I shook hands with people who had never stood in a courtroom or a cell but treated me like I belonged.

And the wildest part? I did.

I gave speeches. Trained new reps. Collected bonus checks and monthly residuals. For the first time since the military, I felt like I was part of something that was building instead of breaking.

Excel changed the way I saw business. It planted the seed that I could be more than an employee. I could be an owner. A visionary. A leader.

"I didn't climb out of prison just to survive. I climbed to lead."

The Fall of Excel — and the Rise of Me

But success has a shelf life. Excel got bought out. Residuals dried up. The company vanished — but I didn't.

Because now, I had the blueprint. I knew I could win. I had built something once — and I could do it again.

That fire inside me? Still burning. That sense of mission? Still focused.

I didn't know it yet, but everything — the hustle, the leadership, the vision — was setting the stage for what would come next:

My invention. My company. My redemption.

What was more valuable than money at Excel Communications during that time wasn't just the commission checks or the flashy perks—it was the mindset training. In those early days, we were introduced to a new way of thinking, and the foundation of that came from the books they recommended.

The Power of the Subconscious Mind by Dr. Joseph Murphy and **Think and Grow Rich** by Napoleon Hill weren't just motivational reads—they were manuals for personal transformation.

These books didn't just teach us how to sell or climb the ranks. They challenged us to look within ourselves and confront the self-limiting beliefs we carried. They taught us that the thoughts we repeated, the vision we held in our minds, and the emotions we connected to our goals could quite literally shape our reality. That wasn't something I grew up hearing in Trenton. It was a whole different language.

For me, this was the turning point—not just professionally, but personally. It gave me a new lens through which to view leadership. Leadership wasn't about titles or barking orders. It was about clarity of vision, consistency in action, and belief in others—especially those who couldn't yet believe in themselves.

Those lessons helped me develop the confidence to work with people from all walks of life, to coach and uplift, and to build teams that didn't just function, but thrived. I started to see the power of planting seeds in others—seeds of potential, of self-worth, of growth.

That period in Excel became a masterclass not in business, but in becoming. And long after the calls ended and the conference rooms emptied, those books remained with me, continuing to shape the man I was becoming.

I hit the ground running.

During my time with Excel Communications, I wasn't just participating—I was building a legacy.

I had independent representatives in my downline from up and down the East Coast and beyond. Folks from New York to Florida, even as far west as Texas, were joining under my leadership.

I was a Regional Training Director and a Regional

Director, yes, but more than that, I was part of a wave that was changing lives.

I had the chance to rub elbows with some of the biggest names in the company.

Steve Smith pictured here with me, the very first independent representative personally recruited by the founder, Kenny Troutt, made a lasting impression on me.

Then there was the late **Paul Orberson,** who at one point was earning an astonishing $900,000 a month from Excel.

This wasn't just a business—it was a phenomenon. Celebrities were joining. People from every walk of life saw what we saw: a chance to change their lives.

And I was in the center of it all—shaking hands, building teams, and speaking to crowds hungry for what we were offering.

That season of my life built more than income. It built

confidence, discipline, and connections that would echo through everything I pursued afterward.I built a strong downline, and not just with anybody.

My team included two professional fighters from
**Trenton, New Jersey: "The Fighting Preacher" Kilpatric
Mitchell**, and

**Bryant "B.B." Brannon, the NABF Super
Middleweight Champion.**

Bryant's brothers, **Charlie "Cho Cho" Boston** and **Jesse
Boston**, came from a legendary local lineage. Their father,
Charles "Tex" Boston, wasn't just a neighborhood name—he
was the stuff of urban folklore.

Charles "Tex" Boston once punched a cow in the head
and knocked it out cold.

That story wasn't just rumor—it was told to me firsthand
by **Lyndsey Page,** a respected former fighter, Army veteran,
correctional officer, and **International boxing referee** who said
he witnessed it himself at **Jones Farm.**

That kind of toughness, passed through generations, was the same spirit I brought to my hustle in Excel. I worked my way up the ranks and earned the title of Regional Director and Regional Training Director.

I didn't just build a business—I taught others how to win. I trained new reps, ran leadership calls, and led from the front.I traveled, I mentored, and I even met the company's billionaire owner, **Kenny Trout**. My success became a symbol—proof that even someone with a record could rise. Here's me with

top money earner **Al Thomas** my upline and my downline superstar **Mark Finney.**

Al Thomas was making about $700,000 a month back then.

Here's some pictures of **New York Giants Star Curtis McGriff Defensive End** during the 1980's doing Excel during the 1990's. When Excel was later acquired and the opportunity faded, I didn't. The flame inside me stayed lit. And I knew I had more to do.

CHAPTER FIVE:

THE PIVOT

. . . .

As time went on, my mother's side of the family slowly stopped getting together the way we used to. The large gatherings, cookouts, and impromptu visits that once defined our close-knit bonds became less frequent. After I got married in the 1990s, I began attending family reunions on my father's side down in Charlottesville, Virginia. It was refreshing to connect with relatives I hadn't known well growing up and to get reacquainted with the Southern roots I came from. We made an effort to meet every year or two, and for the most part, we stayed consistent.

Coming from the fast-paced city life of Trenton, New Jersey, being immersed in the country lifestyle of Virginia felt like a breath of fresh air. The peace, the open land, and most of all, the hospitality and love shown by my aunts, uncles, and cousins made every visit feel like a homecoming. We laughed, shared stories, played music, and broke bread together—those reunions were truly healing and grounding experiences.

One year, after my brother Kevin came home from prison, I decided to bring him with me to the family reunion for the first time. That trip turned into something memorable. During the reunion, my cousin Barry grabbed the microphone and started freestyling—his performance was raw, passionate, and undeniably talented. His sister Lisa came to me afterward and asked if I would help him with his music career. At the time, I had no idea how to manage an artist, but I said yes that I would try to help him. Eventually, I became the manager of **Bee Phox**, as Barry called himself on the mic. Watching my brother **Kevin** being embraced by the family was one of the best parts of that trip—everyone was glad to see him, and the love he received was genuine.

What stood out about my father's side of the family was how deeply rooted and organized they were when it came to tracing our heritage. They took immense pride in knowing our history. In fact, **The Daily Progress**, a local Charlottesville newspaper, published a piece on my **first cousin Paul C. Harris,** who had made history as a former delegate representing Virginia's 58th District—ironically, the same legislative seat once held by Thomas Jefferson. Through family research and interviews, we discovered that our roots stretch all the way back to the grounds of Monticello.

My **Aunt Sylvia Coles, our unofficial family historian**, strongly believes that we are descendants of the enslaved people who lived and worked on **Jefferson's plantation.** Two **Charlottesville authors, Lucia "Cinder" Stanton of Monticello** and **historian Henry S. Wiencek**—known for his work on the **legacy of slavery** at Mount Vernon and Monticello —uncovered records suggesting a **Harris ancestor** may have been enslaved by a **Monticello caretaker in the 1860s.** While the tie is not yet fully documented, the mounting evidence is compelling and has reshaped how we understand our family legacy.

We are now formally acknowledged as **Gatekeepers at Monticello**—a powerful recognition that honors the enduring presence and contributions of our ancestors on that land. I carry this honor with deep pride, representing not only myself but also my late father, who is no longer here. All of his siblings and their descendants are included in this designation. We have lifetime membership and are welcomed at Monticello not just as visitors, but as keepers of history and living descendants of the enslaved who helped build that legacy. It is both humbling and empowering to know that our family's story is now woven into the very narrative of that historic place.

During this same period, I was introduced to another multi-level marketing (MLM) company called Youngevity.

The company had a unique pitch: they were helping people shop online through a platform called Aisle 19, which allowed members to receive discounts on everyday products, including health supplements and even Voice over Internet Protocol (VoIP) phone services. On paper, it seemed promising—another opportunity to leverage network marketing to build a business and help others do the same.

But unlike Excel Communications or other MLM ventures I had been involved with, Youngevity just didn't capture the same energy or marketing momentum. The concept was a little ahead of its time, especially for people not yet accustomed to shopping online in the way we do today. Despite the potential, I found myself spinning my wheels—putting in effort, making calls, trying to build a team, but seeing very little progress or return. I gave it a fair shot, but eventually I had to step away. It might still be around today, but for me, it became clear that this particular venture wasn't the path forward.

After everything I had been through—conflict, prison, broken dreams, and redemption—I found myself drawn to something I never expected: a camera.

Then, Cool Hugh Video came to life…

I started a video service called **Cool Hugh Video**. Just me, a camcorder, and a growing hunger to capture life, frame by frame. I was a self-taught freelance videographer, mostly shooting weddings, parties, baby showers, and milestone celebrations—moments people would want to remember forever. Maybe it was because I had lost so many of my own.

There was something healing in filming joy.

In seeing people come together to dance, to cry, to toast the good things.

Maybe I couldn't save every memory of my own past, but I could help someone else preserve theirs.

Suddenly, I was back to square one.

I had tasted what it felt like to build something of my own, and I wanted that again.

So I started looking for my own business, something I could control from top to bottom—no buyouts, no broken promises. That's when I picked up a camera. It felt natural. Free. Like I could tell stories without having to say a word.

I picked up a lot on my own—lighting tricks, angles, editing cuts—but I also wanted to sharpen my skills. So in 2010, I decided to go back to school and took a video production course at **Mercer County Community College.** That was right after one of the deepest personal losses of my life: the death of my baby brother, **Kevin Brian Harris,** in 2009.

Losing Kevin broke something in me—and rebuilt something else.

He had always looked up to me. And in that moment of grief, I realized I had a choice: I could sink... or I could create.

Cool Hugh Video became more than just a hustle.

It became a tribute.

It was after receiving another inheritance that I was finally able to fund Cool Hugh Video and start working as an independent contractor. That move gave me a sense of stability I hadn't had in a long time.

Every wedding I filmed felt like a silent promise to Kevin that I wouldn't waste another minute. Every frame was a reminder that life keeps going—whether or not we're ready for it. And I had a responsibility to capture it in the best light possible.

Eventually, people started knowing my name—not as someone from "the old days" but as "the guy with the camera." I shot everything from birthday celebrations to community events, and even a few local music videos. I had found a way to stay behind the scenes, but still play a role in people's most important moments.

I took this picture at my former job of **Karen Domino White** she had heard about a picture hanging on the wall right behind her in this image of her father **Fats Domino.**

While building Cool Hugh Video in 2011, I was carrying a weight most people couldn't see. Going back, just two years earlier, in 2009, was when I had suffered an unimaginable series of losses, all passed away one after another, back to back to back. I was still reeling from the shock when, in 2011, the most painful blow came:

Have you ever watched someone take their final breaths on a ventilator. The machine keep going for a while, but you know that they're slipping away. Saying goodbye while still hooked up, it was one of the hardest things I've ever had to do. It broke me in a way I couldn't describe. It broke all of us.

Even as I was trying to build something new with Cool Hugh Video, my heart was drowning in grief.

Every step forward felt like walking through quicksand, but I kept pushing. I had to—for them, and for me.

I invested in equipment—tripods, wireless mics, editing software, upgraded camcorders—thinking I was securing my future as a reliable professional. But what I didn't see coming was the quiet competition creeping up in everyone's back pocket: the iPhone.

At first, I didn't think much of it. I figured people still wanted quality. They still wanted someone who knew how to frame a shot, capture the right light, tell a story through the lens. But over time, I started hearing, "We're just gonna film it ourselves," or "My cousin's got the new iPhone, it takes great video."

I had spent years building this craft, only to realize the game had changed while I was chasing the dream. I took this picture of **Rocky Lockridge** at **Joe Frazier's Funeral.**

Joe Frazier was related to my first cousin's grandmother **Liz** on his mother **Martha** side by marriage. Here with her mother Liz.

Still, I didn't give up. What I offered wasn't just gear—it was vision, experience, and passion. An iPhone could record the moment. I captured the meaning.

Cool Hugh Video may not have become a media empire, but it was a stepping stone. It taught me the power of seeing life through a new lens—literally and figuratively.

It gave me a voice without needing to be in front of the camera. And more importantly, it taught me to adapt, stay creative, and never stop evolving.

Because when you're a survivor, every chapter becomes a lesson.

And every lens—no matter how small—has the power to tell a story that changes lives.I was still grinding—still creating.

Cool Hugh Video was my next evolution, giving a platform to the culture, the community, and the creatives around me. I was producing, directing, and networking with artists and entertainers. It was another way to stay relevant, visible, and engaged.

Several years later, while still pushing forward with Cool Hugh Video, I found myself in a conversation that would change everything. I was working as an independent contractor, and during one of my jobs, I got to talking with an associate who happened to be a former Air Force Veteran.

As we were talking about life, the military came up. He looked at me and said something that stopped me in my tracks: "You might be a Disabled American Veteran and not even know it."

His ex-wife had worked for the VA, and he told me he'd get a number from her for me to call. A few days later, he came through and handed me the contact info. That simple gesture opened the door to a truth I hadn't known for over two decades.

That recognition wouldn't just give me a title—it would give me the residual income I had earned long ago but never received. It would give me validation.

Whatever you believe in—or even if you don't—find something that drives you. Something that makes you want to leave a mark. Keep going. Don't ever give up. And above all, don't let pride get in the way. Stay humble.

I had served during the **Lebanon Crisis** and **Grenada's Operation Urgent Fury.** I had done my time, been **honorably discharged**—and yet, I never realized that the physical and emotional toll I carried made me eligible for veterans' disability benefits. That phone call would set in motion a journey toward recognition, support, and healing that had been long overdue.

The Backbone of My Journey

Throughout all the chaos and change, family remained the anchor that kept me grounded. My sister **Wetonah Carter** had **eleven children** and about **thirty grandchildren** — a large, loving family that I have always been deeply concerned about and protective of. They remind me of the importance of legacy and responsibility.

Faith was another pillar. Even when I didn't always understand the path I was on, I believed there was a higher purpose for my life. That belief kept me moving forward through dark times.

Focus became a daily practice. With so much noise around me — loss, temptation, setbacks — I learned to lock in on what mattered: healing, growth, and progress.

Family, faith, and focus — these three things kept me from falling back into old habits. They became the foundation for the man I was becoming.

I had seen the world.

I had faced death.

I had worn the uniform with pride.

And yet, as far as the world was concerned, I was just another Black man with a short haircut and no direction.

No Map for the Mission

The transition from soldier to civilian hit me harder than boot camp ever did. When I left Trenton, I had a duffel bag and a dream. When I returned, I had scars, some savings, and no blueprint.

No one explained the process. No one sat me down and said, *"Here's what you're entitled to as a veteran."* No mention of the **GI Bill**, no info about **VA healthcare**, and definitely no word about **service-connected disability**.

I didn't know it yet, but I was already a **disabled veteran**, carrying internal injuries the Army hadn't fully addressed. After I had undergone **surgery**, and they told me flat out, *"You'll never run again."* That cut deep—not just physically, but mentally. Running was how I cleared my head, how I released stress. It was freedom. And now it was gone.

I was only **thirty years old**, and they were already telling me what I'd never do again.

But they didn't know me.

Job to Job—Check to Check

I tried to stay afloat the legit way. I worked **odd jobs**, construction, delivery gigs, a little warehouse work. I didn't complain—I worked. But the math never worked out.

Rent. Groceries. Gas. Survival.

The numbers didn't add up.

I was a trained soldier with leadership experience, but employers looked at me like I was a **risk, not an asset**. I had to hustle just to **look employed**, let alone stay employed.

At one point, I was crashing at a crowded apartment, barely scraping by. The refrigerator was half-empty, and the air was always tense. Pride kept me from asking for help, but deep down I was **exhausted**. Exhausted from trying to be strong. Exhausted from pretending I was okay.

2009 hit me like a series of body blows—each loss heavier than the last. It was a devastating year that tested my strength and spirit in ways I never expected. The first blow came when my cousin **Jennifer** passed away. That loss was sudden and heartbreaking. Jennifer had a light about her—a warmth that pulled people in. Her absence was felt deeply and immediately.

Then came another gut punch that summer. In July, my Uncle James—one of my mother's twin brothers, James and Jerome—passed away. Around 2005, **Uncle James** had lived with us for a while when he needed a place to stay. We welcomed him in like family should. Eventually, he got back on his feet and moved out, managing on his own for a few years.

But in 2008, Uncle James was diagnosed with lung cancer. It was a hard diagnosis for all of us to accept. During that time, my sister Wetonah stepped up in a big way. She became his primary caregiver, looking after him with compassion, strength, and consistency. She was there through the hospital visits, the treatments, and the long nights. Watching her care for him like that made me proud—it reminded me what family really means when everything else falls away.

In 2009, after everything he had fought through, **Uncle James passed away**. Kevin and I had previously sent him a return ticket to come back to New Jersey from Arizona, where he'd been hit by a car while walking. We wanted him home, close to family, so we could take care of him. But before that could happen, he was gone. It hurt in a way that's hard to describe—not just because we lost him, but because we'd come so close to helping him start fresh.

And then in **September 2009,** I lost my brother **Kevin.**

Kevin had come home from prison in **2001,** and from the moment he returned, he was determined to get back on track. He stayed with me, and he was a great addition to the family—reliable, focused, and driven to do better. He didn't just talk about turning things around—he lived it. Kevin worked two jobs at the same time, hustling the right way, showing that it was never too late to make a change.

We shared our space, our stories, and our mutual desire to rise above our pasts. His dedication inspired me and reminded all of us of the power of redemption.

Losing him felt like losing more than a brother—it was like losing a living testimony of what transformation could look like. He had so much more life to live, and we were proud of the man he was becoming. His passing left a silence in my life that still lingers.

As if that wasn't enough, in April **2011,** my mother, **Alice J. Harris,** passed away.

That loss was devastating in a way only a child can truly understand. No matter how old you are, when your mother leaves this world, you lose a part of yourself that can't be replaced.

But through it all, once again, my sister Wetonah showed what strength really looks like. Along with her children, she became our mother's caregiver in her final stretch. They took care of her around the clock, making sure she was surrounded by love, comfort, and dignity. They gave her what every mother deserves: peace in her final days and the presence of the people she loved most.

Watching them come together as a unit reminded me that even through unbearable loss, the love of family is what keeps us grounded. Through every tragedy, there was someone showing up—not for recognition, but because it was the right thing to do. That's what family means to me.

The emergence of crack cocaine in Los Angeles gave rise to what the public and the media viewed as an epidemic of alarming proportions. As crack cocaine began to proliferate throughout the country in the 1980s, public fear of the devastating new drug, instigated by sensationalist media coverage, was widespread. The political dialogue surrounding the crack epidemic was equally sensationalistic.

Public frenzy surrounding crack cocaine peaked in **June 1986,** when **Len Bias**—a basketball superstar at the University of Maryland—died of a tragic overdose just two days after the Boston Celtics drafted him second overall in the NBA draft.

Congress recognized the legitimate public health and safety concerns raised by crack cocaine shortly after Bias died, and a bipartisan consensus emerged to craft a legislative response—**the Anti-Drug Abuse Act of 1986 (ADAA).**

In less than a decade, the United States Sentencing Commission (Sentencing Commission) concluded that the ADAA was premised on faulty assumptions about crack, produced anomalous disparities in federal cocaine sentencing, and had a vastly disproportionate impact on **African Americans.** Despite mounting concerns about the ADAA sentencing regime, the ADAA mandatory minimums remained federal cocaine sentencing policy for twenty-four years, until Congress passed the **Fair Sentencing Act of 2010 (FSA).**

Through the FSA, Congress prospectively amended the ADAA mandatory minimums by increasing the threshold drug quantity required to trigger the statutory minimums—replacing the 100-to-1 sentencing ratio with an 18-to-1 ratio. The FSA also directed the Sentencing Commission to promulgate emergency amendments to the Sentencing Guidelines (Guidelines) to reflect the new, comparatively lenient FSA power-to-crack quantity ratio.

The Sentencing Commission promulgated these amendments and subsequently decided to apply them retroactively. The retroactive amendments allowed for Guidelines offenders—that is, prisoners sentenced to Guidelines sentences above or below the ADAA mandatory minimums—to obtain minor sentence reductions pursuant to 18 U.S.C. § 3582(c)(2). This really had an impact on my situation.

Although the Sentencing Commission applied the newly promulgated Guidelines retroactively, Congress did not include an express statement of retroactivity in the FSA to apply the newly enacted mandatory minimums retroactively. Unless it was the "fair implication" of Congress to apply the FSA retroactively, the saving statute triggers a legal presumption that the remedial amendments to the ADAA mandatory minimums apply prospectively.

Because the Sentencing Commission lacks authority to alter the statutory minimums, and the FSA does not contain an express statement of retroactivity, prisoners currently serving ADAA mandatory minimum sentences—unlike their counterparts serving Guidelines sentences—are ineligible for retroactive sentence reductions based on the newly enacted FSA mandatory minimums.

To further complicate this legal landscape, in 2012, the Supreme Court held that the FSA is, in a sense, partially retroactive, in that the Act's mandatory minimums apply to crack offenders arrested before but sentenced after the passage of the FSA.

Nonetheless, the prevailing interpretation of the FSA, unanimously endorsed by the federal circuit courts of appeals, is that the FSA mandatory minimums do not apply retroactively for the purpose of discretionary sentence-modification proceedings under § 3582(c)(2). Faith the size of a mustard seed will hold you!

Courts addressing the issue of retroactivity—most notably the Sixth Circuit in United States v. Blewett (Blewett II)—have expressed serious constitutional concerns about categorically denying ADAA mandatory minimum offenders the opportunity to obtain sentence reductions while allowing similarly situated Guidelines offenders to obtain the same relief. Music to my ears!

This Comment provides an in-depth overview of federal cocaine sentencing policy and analyzes the practical and constitutional concerns raised by the prevailing interpretation of the FSA mandatory minimums.

This Comment contends that permitting the remedial amendments to the ADAA mandatory minimums to apply retroactively at discretionary sentence-modification proceedings would further the six purposes of the FSA—as evidenced by the legislative history of the FSA, overwhelming congressional opposition to pre-FSA cocaine sentencing policy, and secondary policy considerations.

It further argues that courts denying discretionary retroactive effect to the FSA mandatory minimums have undermined the policy objectives of the FSA by misguidedly breathing life into the discriminatory **100-to-1 sentencing ratio** for purposes of sentence-modification proceedings.

This Comment concludes that the FSA's mandatory minimums should be applied retroactively at discretionary sentence-modification proceedings because the failure to do so is inconsistent with the recent overhaul of federal drug sentencing policy and constitutional principles of equal protection.

Trying to Love While Drowning

Relationships? Man… they were rough.

After my divorce from my ex-wife **Donna**, I was emotionally fractured. I kept looking for comfort in the wrong places—sometimes old flames, sometimes new ones I wasn't ready for.

I don't know if it was my **financial situation**, or the weight of my **unresolved trauma**, but I couldn't seem to make anything last. I was emotionally unavailable half the time and too wounded to admit it.

There was one woman I tried to build with after breaking up with another ex. She had a **young son and a dog**. She was going through her own struggle and ended up **homeless so she said**. I let her move in with me, even though I was already living in a packed house with barely enough room to turn around.

We tried to make it work. But she wasn't being fully honest about her situation, and I wasn't fully healed. After a few wasted years, it all unraveled. Another lesson learned the hard way.

Another Hustle, Another Shot

Prior to this period, I got involved with another **multi-level marketing** company—**Youngevity**.

They were selling **nutritional supplements**, internet services, and a shopping portal called **Aisle 19**, where you could get rebates and discounts by buying everyday products.

It sounded promising at first. It reminded me of my earlier days with **Excel Communications**, where I had real traction, real team-building, and even became a **Regional Training Director**. But this time, the wheels just spun. The product didn't move. The message didn't catch.

I wanted to believe. I always did. But after a while, belief wasn't enough. I needed results.

The Birth of Cool Hugh Video

It was after receiving a small **inheritance**—another blessing I hadn't expected—that I was able to **start Cool Hugh Video**. I bought some basic camera equipment, started freelancing, and got gigs recording events, parties, and small projects. It wasn't glamorous, but it was mine.

That's when I met a man named **Willie**. He wasn't flashy. He wasn't loud. But he gave me something more valuable than money.

He gave me **information**.

A Life-Changing Discovery

Willie was the one who looked me in the eye and asked, "Did you ever file for **service-connected disability**?"

I said no.

He said, "You served during **Lebanon and Grenada**, right?"

I nodded.

He said, "Brother, you might be sitting on **something life-changing.** You're a disabled vet and you don't even know it."

It was like someone had just told me I had gold buried in my own backyard.

I followed up. I got documentation. I sat with a **Veteran Service Officer.** I reopened my file, pulled my medical records, showed my medical history. And slowly, things started to shift.

I started receiving benefits I had earned decades ago—**money, healthcare, resources**—things that should have been mine all along.

It wasn't charity. It was justice.

Don't Block Your Blessings

Looking back, I understand something I didn't back then:

Sometimes your blessing doesn't come in the form of **money** or **opportunity**. Sometimes your blessing comes in the form of a **person who points you in the right direction.**

Willie didn't give me a dollar.

He gave me **knowledge**.

And knowledge changed my life.

He helped me walk through the right door at the right time, and for the first time in years—I could **breathe**.

New Strength, New Purpose

Now I wasn't just surviving—I was building. I had enough stability to **look ahead**, to **plan**, to **dream again**. That's when the early ideas for **Reyena** started whispering in the back of my mind. But that journey would come later.

Right now, I was just grateful to feel **seen**. To know that after all the loss, after all the rejection, **my service had meant something**.

I wasn't just a vet.

I wasn't just a survivor.

I was becoming a man with purpose again.

I had come home.

I had hustled again.

But now, I was finally ready to build something permanent.

CHAPTER SIX:

THE RISE OF REYENA

Some inventions are born in labs. Others are born in heartbreak, frustration, and the relentless need to **make sense out of survival**.

Reyena didn't start as a product.

It started as a **question**: Why didn't I have proof?

Why didn't I have footage to show I wasn't at fault?

Why didn't I have audio to back up my version of events?

Why didn't I have the kind of **evidence** that could have saved me—and others—from being criminalized, dismissed, or ignored?

That question stayed with me for **years**. Through job losses. Through wrongful stops. Through family court, street fights, shady police encounters, and courtroom drama. Every time someone lied on me or misrepresented what happened, I wished I had **receipts**.

And then I thought…

What if we could build the receipts right into the ride?

Every Road Was a Memory

I had driven all kinds of cars in my life—old beaters, borrowed Buicks, rental vans, and even borrowed hot rods from time to time. But every time I got behind the wheel, I felt two things: **freedom and fear**.

Freedom because driving meant motion—progress, escape, possibility.

Fear because one wrong move, one lie, one false charge, and I could lose everything.

I had been stopped by police for reasons that made no sense. I had seen **good people lose their licenses, their jobs, and even their lives** over traffic stops gone wrong. I had seen **crooked cops and shaky stories**, and I had nothing to fight back with but my word.

And sometimes, your word ain't enough.

I needed something smarter, something faster, and something made for people like us.

The Idea Hit Like Lightning

I was riding with a friend one day—he was speeding. We were laughing, talking about life, and then suddenly... red and blue lights. Cop walks up, says we were doing 73 in a 50.

Now my boy had a radar detector on the dash, and he swore we weren't going that fast.

But there was no **proof**. No timestamp. No footage. No audio. Just **his word against the badge**.

It hit me then:

What if we had a **device** that could record your speed, **show the time, record the conversation, see all angles,** and even **stream live** if something went down?

A dashcam wasn't enough.

A radar detector wasn't enough.

A livestream wasn't enough.

But **all three**—and more—in **one unit**?

Now *that* could change lives.

The Vision Was Born: Reyena

The name came to me like a whisper: **Reyena.**

It sounded like a woman. Strong. Protective. A guardian. A witness. The kind of presence you wish you had with you in every moment that could change your life.

But Reyena wasn't just a name. It became a mission.

A patented, all-in-one system that would do what no single device could:

- ✅ Record all around the car with **four synchronized cameras**

- ✅ Capture **speed**, **location**, and **sound** with timestamped evidence

- ✅ Feature a **radar detector** that not only warns—but **documents**

- ✅ Offer touchscreen navigation, Bluetooth, WiFi, and app control

- ✅ Enable **Facebook Live streaming** directly from the cloud

- ✅ Be invisible to cops and empowering to drivers

This wasn't about technology. This was about **accountability**.

Why I Had to Build It

I wasn't just trying to make money. I was trying to make a **weapon for truth**.

I thought about all the young brothers pulled over with no witnesses. All the mothers fighting to protect their kids from false accusations. All the fathers like me—fighting for their name, their dignity, their legacy.

Reyena would be the **silent witness**.

The one that never blinks.

The one that never forgets.

The one that never lies.

If I had Reyena back in the day, half the trouble I'd been through wouldn't have happened. The lies wouldn't have stuck. The trauma wouldn't have repeated. And I wouldn't have had to fight so many invisible battles.

So I knew: If no one else builds it—I will.

From Idea to Action

I started sketching. Writing down specs. Imagining where the cameras would go. How the radar sensor would integrate. Where the speed stamp would be displayed in **August 2016.**

I started calling people, asking questions, researching patents. I didn't have engineering experience, but I had **real-world knowledge**. I had pain and purpose. I had vision. I was told no to my idea for an invention by a intellectual property attorney in **2017**

And that's when I connected with **Lisa Ascolese later on in 2018**, known in the industry as **"The Inventress."** She had launched products on **HSN** and **QVC**, had a track record of turning **ideas into reality**, and she believed in people like me.

I told her about Reyena. She leaned in and said, *"That's brilliant."*

That was all I needed.

She introduced me to the legal team at **Gearhart Law**, and before I knew it, we were filing **patents**, building prototypes, and getting trademarks. I even secured the domain **reyena.org**, began crafting a logo, and started putting together **mockups** and presentation decks.

For the first time in my life—I wasn't just reacting to the world.

I was creating one.

A Product With a Pulse

Reyena wasn't just a device—it was a **movement**.

It stood for every moment where the truth wasn't enough.

For every life lost to silence.

For every unjust charge, misrepresented stop, and ignored claim.

It stood for **Shawn**—my nephew.

It stood for **Aaron**, who fought so hard to live.

It stood for **myself**—and the hundreds of men and women like me who survived long enough to invent a better way.

And here's the truth: **I'm not a tech guy.**

I'm not Silicon Valley.

I'm not a coder, or a millionaire, or a guy with an Ivy League team behind me.

But I have something more powerful:

Experience. Truth. And a reason.

Legacy in the Making

I once stood in the middle of a burning house and barely made it out.

I once stood in a prison cell wondering if I'd ever have a second chance.

I once stood broke, broken, and overlooked.

But now—

I stand behind **Reyena**.

I stand behind a product that can **save lives, protect truth**, and **hold power accountable**.

That's not just invention.

That's redemption.

Reyena isn't just mine.

It belongs to every voice that was silenced.

Every life that deserved a second angle.

Every driver that needed one more witness.

And every person who still believes…

that truth is worth protecting.

In 2019, I made one of the boldest moves of my life—I filed a provisional and utility patent application through Gearhart Law. The filing cost me $5,200, and it wasn't just a business move. It was a personal declaration that I was no longer living in the past—I was building a future. That year marked a turning point for me. I wasn't just surviving anymore. I was creating. Dreaming. Inventing.

But I knew that if I was serious about becoming an inventor, I had to address the shadow that still lingered over my name—my criminal record. My past. So later that same year, I did something that people told me was nearly impossible: I filed for a Governor's Pardon.

At the time, my convictions weren't even considered pardonable. But I walked out on faith. Humble, but determined. I believed that if I wanted to truly move forward, I had to try—against all odds.

My Attorney, H. Robert Tillman, stood by me through the entire process. He prepared me for every possible outcome—whether good, bad, or inconclusive. His knowledge, candor, and integrity were exactly what I needed in that moment. Outstanding attorney. He didn't sugarcoat anything, but he never let me lose hope either.

Then came COVID-19. The whole world stopped. The court system slowed to a crawl. Hearings were delayed, paperwork stalled, and everything that once felt like progress now felt suspended in midair. But I made a personal proclamation right then and there: I'm in this for the long haul. For the invention. For the pardon. For my future.

I had also started hearing whispers—rumblings about the crack-to-cocaine disparity finally being addressed. **The Fair Sentencing Act and the First Step Act** were being talked about more and more. I paid close attention. I had been sentenced on two second-degree charges for possession with intent to distribute crack cocaine, and I knew firsthand how harsh and imbalanced those sentences had been compared to powder cocaine offenses.

The **First Step Act**, formally known as the **Formerly Incarcerated Reenter Society Transformed Safely Transitioning Every Person Act**, is a bipartisan criminal justice bill passed by the 115th U.S. Congress and signed by President Donald Trump in December 2018.

The act enacted several changes in U.S. federal criminal law aimed at reforming federal prisons and sentencing laws in order to reduce recidivism, decreasing the federal inmate population, and maintaining public safety.

Then, in July 2019, I learned that the First Step Act was retroactive—it could actually reduce mandatory minimum sentences and change outcomes based on new thresholds. That was the final push I needed. After being told "no" by a different attorney in the past, I decided to move forward anyway.

I had been told I was wasting my time.

That people like me didn't get pardons. That filing a patent while carrying a criminal record was just dreaming too big. But I did it anyway. Not out of arrogance, but out of belief— belief in my growth, belief in my ideas, and belief that redemption is real, even if the world is slow to recognize it.

When COVID-19 emerged in January 2020, it changed the world overnight. COVID-19 is an infectious disease caused by the SARS-CoV-2 virus. Though first discovered in Wuhan, China, in late 2019, it entered the U.S. public conversation in early 2020 with growing concern and chaos.

While most of the country was forced to shut down, I kept pushing forward. I continued working as an independent contractor, delivering food to the public six to seven days a week. It was dangerous work at times, but it gave me purpose. Even with the uncertainty around me, I still had obligations to fulfill—I was actively filing motions with the **United States Patent and Trademark Office,** making modifications to my patent application. I was also continuing to pay separately for my pardon application. COVID didn't stop my progress. It simply added another layer to the grind.

Then in **2021**, I was approached with an unexpected opportunity that reignited another passion of mine—boxing alongside Coach Kilpatric Mitchell and legendary Philadelphia cut-man Fred Jenkins, with promotions handled by Russell Peltz and the late Joe Hand—both well-respected figures in the Philadelphia boxing scene.

While juggling that, I was still working at least five days a week. Life didn't slow down. If anything, it picked up.

In **April 2021**, while I was still waiting to hear back about my executive pardon, I filed for a **Clean Slate Expungement**. It was another attempt to move forward and clear my name—one more piece in the puzzle of reclaiming my life. But everything was moving slowly.

The court system was completely **backed up due to COVID-19**. People were dying left and right—family members, friends, community pillars. You couldn't even visit them in the hospital to say goodbye. The world was grieving in isolation.

During that time, I honestly believed that my invention—my pending patent—would help make a difference in my pardon process. I thought maybe if they saw I was trying to build something meaningful for society, it would help tip the scales. But **that's not what happened**. I still didn't have a finished product. I was still **patent pending**, and to this day I remain **pending on three separate patents**.

Just know, at that point in my life, I was trying everything. Filing, fighting, and moving forward through grief, red tape, and faith.

In **April 2022**, while attending the funeral of a family member, I had another life-shifting moment. One of the siblings of the deceased—someone I had always respected—approached me and asked if I would help manage his rap career.

Before she passed, his sister had expressed her wish that someone would help her little brother stay focused and grounded. He happened to be a fellow veteran too. I said yes without hesitation.

He had saved money, and we decided to invest equally. We hired a lawyer, got the paperwork done, and got to work. This venture all unfolded while I was still actively working as a boxing second trainer and holding down a regular work schedule.

In the middle of all of that, I also tried to find some balance in my personal life. In **July 2022**, my then-fiancée and I took our first cruise together. We came back with more than memories—we tested positive for COVID-19.

We're no longer together now, and maybe that's for the best. Still, the experience reminded me that even the best-laid plans can take unexpected turns.

But through it all, I kept moving. Kept evolving. Whether it was boxing, music, mentorship, or chasing my entrepreneurial goals—I stayed in motion. And even when I caught COVID, I didn't let it break my stride.

CHAPTER SEVEN:

WHEN THE BELL RINGS

Boxing isn't just about fists—it's about focus.

State of New York
Department of State
State Athletic Commission

Professional Boxing Second/Trainer

A license has been granted under Article 41 of the
General Business Law to the following:

Hugh Carter

License Number: DOS-PRO-BOX-SEC-LIC-2024-080241
Effective Date: 06/10/2022
Expiration Date: 06/09/2023

It's about silence between punches, discipline between rounds, and the unspoken bond between the fighter and the one in his corner.

Most people only see the man inside the ring.

But I was never just watching the fights—I was inside the storm, in the corner, one voice in the chaos saying, *"Keep going."*

I wasn't a licensed fighter. But I worked the corners.

Wrapped hands. Watched feet. Wiped sweat. Caught blood. Gave calm.

Because in boxing—just like in life—you need someone in your corner who's been through hell and can still think straight when the bell rings.

How I Got in the Ring Without Throwing a Punch

My entry into professional boxing wasn't planned. December 2021 I was asked to become a partner with **The Fighting Preacher Professional Boxing Coach Kilpatric Mitchell** from the Blue Line Gym to help with **Professional Boxer Quadeer Jenkins.**

I became a **Licensed Professional Boxing Second Trainer** in the State of **New York** in 2022 and **Pennsylvania** working the corner for 4 professional fights with **Coach Mitchell** and cut man **Fred Jenkins** from Philadelphia and **Russell Peltz Promotions** and also the late **Joe Hand Promotions** both from Philadelphia in 2022 while still working at least 5 days a week.

It wasn't part of some long career vision. Like most of the chapters in my life, it started with a connection—someone who knew someone—and next thing I knew, I was **backstage** giving real-time advice to real-deal warriors.

Some of the boxers were seasoned pros. Others were up-and-comers just looking for a shot. All of them were fighting for more than just belts—they were fighting for **rent, pride, legacy, and redemption.**

I knew that feeling well.

So when I stepped into those locker rooms, I didn't just see athletes—I saw **soldiers**. Just like me.

Respect in the Ring

You learn fast in this game: it's not about how loud you talk, it's about how well you **listen**. In boxing, everyone's got ego—but the real ones don't talk much.

They train.

They focus.

They execute.

I spent time with trainers, cut-men, matchmakers, and old-school fight vets who had seen it all. And I kept my ears open.

You'd be surprised how much wisdom flows in a gym that smells like sweat, leather, and liniment oil. Old timers dropping gems between shadowboxing rounds. Fighters quoting Scripture between stretches. Trainers teaching life lessons while wrapping gauze.

Moments That Left a Mark

There were so many nights under the bright lights of small-town arenas, casino halls, and recreation centers packed to the brim. Fans screaming, blood flying, cornermen shouting, and somewhere in the middle of it all—**me**, steady, focused, reminding the fighter to breathe.One night in **Pennsylvania**, I found myself in walking to the ring during introductions and looked across to see none other than **Tim Witherspoon**—the former **two time Heavy Weight Champion of the World**. I shook his hand.

The man who once held the same belts as **Ali**, **Tyson**, and **Holyfield**.

We locked eyes for just a second. He nodded. I nodded back. That moment? That was real. That was respect.

Witherspoon knew I wasn't a tourist. He could see it in how I carried myself. I was there to **serve the fighter**, not shine in the spotlight.

Fighters I Knew, Fighters I Lost

Boxing, like life, is full of glory—and grief.

I cornered fighters who went on to **win**, and I stood beside others who **never fought again** after one devastating loss. I saw men get knocked out and come back stronger, and others get knocked out of their whole career.

Some nights we left with victory.

Other nights we left with towels over our heads, silent and hurting.

But win or lose, I never left their side.

Because that's what you do in a corner. You stay.

The Boxing World Taught Me:

- **Discipline** isn't about perfection—it's about *preparation*.

- **Pain** is a better teacher than praise.

- **Silence** between rounds can say more than shouting.

- And sometimes, you gotta throw in the towel—not because you quit, but because you care.

I saw men get saved by a towel.

I saw others wish someone had cared enough to throw it.

More Than a Sport—A Mirror

Boxing showed me things I already knew from the streets, the Army, and prison—but in a more controlled environment.

- **Footwork** reminded me of how I had to move in the hood: fast, quiet, and strategic.

- **Defense** reminded me of all the times I had to protect myself without ever throwing a punch.

- **Rounds** reminded me that life comes in cycles. You're never down for good—just until the next bell.

And the **corner**?

That reminded me of how important it is to have someone in your life who sees the whole fight and still believes in you.

I had people in my corner. Some visible. Some spiritual. Some who are gone now, but whose voices echo in my head every time I feel like giving up.

The Silent Fights Outside the Ring

What most people don't understand is that **the biggest fight isn't in the ring**—it's outside. It's what happens **after** the lights go off. After the crowd leaves. After the gloves come off.

It's depression.

Addiction.

Injury.

Bills.

Doubt.

That's when you really find out who a fighter is.

And that's why boxing resonated with me.

Because I'd been fighting all my life.

And every round taught me something new.

The bell doesn't end the battle.

It just gives you time to breathe, reset, and swing again!

CHAPTER EIGHT :
FORGING AHEAD WITH
2SOULJIERS AND REYENA

. . . .

Before *Reyena*, before the pardon, before the world even knew my name—I was building something just as powerful, just as personal.

It didn't come with a patent.

It didn't get filed in a law office.

But it carried the same purpose: telling the truth, keeping the record, honoring the voices we weren't supposed to hear.

I'm talking about **hip-hop**.

I'm talking about music as resistance.

I'm talking about **2Souljiers**.

Because before I was an inventor, I was a **witness**. A witness to the pain and power of the hood. A witness to the rhythm of survival. A witness to what happens when young men with vision, trauma, and talent pick up a pen instead of a pistol.

Music Saved Us

I wasn't a rapper. I wasn't a DJ. But I was always **around the music**—in the basements, the corner cyphers, the makeshift studios with mattress foam on the walls and extension cords running out the window.

Music was our therapy. Our escape. Our warning shot. Our way to say, *"We're still here."*

When I partnered with my **first cousin, Bee Phox**, to form **2Souljiers LLC**, it wasn't just about beats and bars. It was about **truth**. We were documenting our era, our city, our struggle. We were the **soundtrack to a generation** that didn't get no parade but still survived the war.

WE CAN DO IT (feat. Unique Songbird & Cool Hugh)

BEE PHOX · WE CAN DO IT (feat. Unique Songbird & Cool Hugh) - Single · May 30, 2024

The 2Souljiers Movement

We didn't have a huge budget.

We didn't have industry connections.

What we had was **fire**.

Bee Phox could spit—**raw, unfiltered, intelligent verses** that told stories the world needed to hear. We spent hours in the studio crafting songs that were **message-driven**, not just commercial.

We released two key singles:

• **"Open Your Mind"** – A wake-up call, calling out materialism, injustice, and spiritual blindness.

• **"We Can Do It"** – An anthem of resilience, reminding the community that unity was still possible.

These tracks weren't just music—they were **mission statements**.

Our website, **2Souljiers.com**, became a hub where people could connect with the movement. No gimmicks. Just **content with conviction**.

Studio Sessions and Sacred Spaces

Some of the most spiritual moments of my life happened **in the studio**. It didn't smell like a church. There was no pulpit. But it was holy. April 2022 at my first cousin Lisa funeral. I was asked by **Bee Phox**, Lisa's baby brother to become his manager for his rap career, before his sister passed away she had asked if i could help her little brother.

We connected with his cousin in law **Jason "Stoneface Miller"** I said okay. He happened to be a veteran too. So I said yes. At this same funeral. I heard a lady sing a tribute for my cousin. **Unique Songbird** would be featured on the second single **"We Can Do It."**

With a powerful message to put down the drugs and guns, that we created a video for with no profanity or twerking against negativity in conjunction with **PAAN** which is the **Philadelphia Anti-Drug/Anti-Violence Network**, that also included me **Cool Hugh** on the ad-lib. We started an **LLC** together called **2Souljiers** with a twist on the spelling.

He had money saved up, so we invested equally and hired a lawyer. All of this was done simultaneously to being a boxing second trainer and working as well. His first single was released in October 2023 after the **Princeton Packet** did a story on us August 2023.

In one session, I remember watching **Bee Phox** lay down a verse in one take—no punch-ins, no edits. He closed his eyes, stood at the mic, and you could see his pain spilling out into the room like incense smoke.

The engineer hit stop and just stared.

That's what truth in real time looks like.

Stoneface: The Blind Producer Who Saw Everything. One of our closest collaborators was **BEE PHOX'S** cousin in law **Jason "Stoneface" Miller**, an incredible artist and producer —and **completely blind**.

Jason wasn't born blind. He lost his vision after a **gunshot wound to the face** at a gas station in Philadelphia.

But instead of letting the trauma define him, he used it to deepen his craft. In the studio, he worked with his ears and heart. And trust me—he heard everything.

He was part of **The Eloheem Team** with **William Cooper**, and his music had a **divine urgency**. You didn't just listen to Stoneface. You **felt** him.

Being in the same room with him was like sitting next to wisdom. He'd say something offhand like, *"Energy don't lie,"* and you'd carry that with you for weeks.

Jason didn't need sight.

He saw more than most men with 20/20 vision.

Legacy Through Loss

We were losing people constantly.

Bee and I talked often about how our music wasn't just for **recognition**—it was for **remembrance**. For the ones who didn't make it. The ones taken by gunfire, prison time, addiction, or the slow fade of depression.

I lost my **nephew Aaron**, who died in prison after contracting an infection at the **same hospital where I almost died once**. That hit hard. That was personal. He had survived the fire as a child—and later died in the flames of the system.

His **sister**—my niece—was found **dead on her couch**, leaving behind a daughter named **Blessing**. These weren't just deaths. These were **cuts to the soul**. Nine days later my uncle **Jerome Carter Sr.** namesake **Jerome Carter Jr.** passed away.

who was also a rap artist. **J. Carter**

When we recorded, their names echoed in every snare hit, every verse, every beat drop.

New Generations, New Waves

Legacy don't stop with one generation.

Later on my **nephew Joe Cartega** launched his own movement: **Only The Real Battle League**

@cartegas_corner@ig. What started as a platform for battling became a **launchpad for lyrical warriors** from Trenton and beyond.

Joe eventually joined a **supergroup called The Momentum,** and they released an album titled **Broken Dreams**. On it, Joe appeared on a powerful track called **"G. Q. J. Interlude"**—a direct nod to his recently departed brother, my nephew **Aaron "Gunz" Carter** who died in prison custody at Helene Fuld Hospital Trenton,NJ.

Hearing his name in the middle of that track? That was the first time I realized... There was **a bridge**.

Not just between generations, but between **struggle and purpose, pain and progress, the past and the possible.**

We Weren't Rappers. We Were Reporters.

People ask, "Were you trying to get signed?"

That was never the point.

We were trying to **get heard**.

We were trying to **document**.

We were trying to **heal**.

Because when the news cameras left, when the press ignored us, when the courts mislabeled us—hip-hop told the truth.

Our microphones were our affidavits.

Our tracks were our testimonies.

Our rhymes were our receipts.

From the Studio to the Streets—and Back Again

We sold CDs hand to hand.

We hit community centers, barbershops, open mics, and block parties.

We built from the bottom—because that's where the truth lives.

Everywhere we went, we met people who didn't need fame. They needed **voice**. And we gave them that. Through rhythm, reflection, and raw honesty.

That's why **2Souljiers** still matters.

It's more than music.

It's ministry.

It's memoir.

It's movement.

In the booth, I found healing.

In the beat, I found memory.

And in the street, I found my purpose.

CHAPTER NINE:
REDEMPTION AND THE
ROAD TO PARDON

. . . .

Redemption doesn't happen overnight.

It's not a flash of light or a single moment of glory.

It's a thousand little decisions made when nobody's looking.

It's choosing humility when you could've chosen revenge.

It's working low-paying jobs with a head full of talent.

It's rebuilding trust with people who have every reason not to believe in you.

Redemption is a grind.

And I earned every scar of it.

But what I didn't know was that one day, my name—the same name that had been whispered, written off, and misjudged—would be cleared.

That one day, the **State of New Jersey** would say: "We were wrong. And we're going to make it right."

The Journey Back

After I got out of prison, I wasn't looking for a parade. I just wanted to move on. But society doesn't let you forget your mistakes.

Every job application.

Every rental form.

Every background check.

The box.

That box.

"Have you ever been convicted of a felony?"

Check it, and the door slams before it even opens.

Lie about it, and you risk losing everything you built.

So I lived in this grey zone—**free, but not really free**.I worked wherever I could. Took side gigs. Kept creating. Kept serving.

I didn't sit around feeling sorry for myself—I hustled forward.

But deep down, I still wanted something more than a second chance.

I wanted restoration.

A Letter I Almost Didn't Write

One day, someone told me about the possibility of a **Governor's Pardon**.

Now if you've never applied for one, let me explain:

It's not just paperwork.

It's a soul statement.

They want your record.

Your letters of recommendation.

Your proof of change.

Your plan for the future.

Your past in black and white.

I almost didn't do it.

Why? Because I had been rejected so many times before.

I was tired of trying to prove to the world I wasn't the same man they locked up.

But something—maybe God, maybe purpose, maybe stubbornness—pushed me to do it.

I filled out every form. Wrote every word myself.

I told the truth—**the full truth**.

Not the prettied-up version.

Not the polished résumé.

Just *me*. Raw. Honest.

A man who had fallen, risen, and wanted the chance to **close the loop**.

The Waiting Game

Once I sent it off, there was nothing left to do but wait.

Weeks turned to months.

I went back to work. I kept building **Reyena**. I stayed quiet.

But I prayed.

I don't talk a lot about religion, but I believe in **timing**.

I believe in seeds taking root.

And I believe that if you move right, God moves too.

So I waited. With faith, but not expectation.

The Call That Changed Everything

Then one day, I got the call.

Governor Phil Murphy, of the State of New Jersey, had **granted me a full pardon. December 16th, 2024.**

My record was not just sealed—it was erased.

Like the system finally exhaled and said, "You did your time. You did the work. And now, you get your name back."

I don't cry often.

But that day?

I broke down.

Not out of sadness.

Out of **release**.

Out of the weight of years—lifted.

Out of the shame I carried for too long—cleared.

Out of the chance to walk into rooms without apology—
finally mine.

What a Pardon Really Means

People think a pardon is about erasing a record.

It's not.

It's about restoring a name.

You can't undo the past. But you can **reframe it**.

You can say, "I did that time, but that time didn't define me."

You can say, "I paid the debt—and I built something greater from it."

With that pardon, I wasn't just a "former felon."

I was a vet, a businessman, an inventor, a mentor, a man fully redeemed.

And let me tell you:

When I held that pardon in my hands, it felt like **a folded flag at a soldier's funeral**—symbolic, weighty, and filled with meaning.

It said, "You are no longer who the system said you were."

Full Circle

To go from being incarcerated and nearly dying…

To being pardoned by a sitting governor?

That's God's math.

That's **proof**.

That you can go through hell and still be worthy of heaven.

That you can be buried by circumstance and still bloom.

And it reminded me—**my story matters.**

Not just to me.

But to every man or woman still waiting for their own call.

Still hoping their name will be cleared.

Still walking the line between guilt and grace.

The Real Victory

This wasn't about headlines.

This was about **legacy**.

Now when I talk to young men trying to beat the streets, I don't speak from theory.

I speak from truth.

- "You can change."

- "You can fall and rise."

- "You can walk through the fire and not be consumed."

- "You can go from prison to purpose."

And now, thanks to that pardon, I don't just tell that story…

I embody it.

The record no longer defines me.

The road I chose does. And I chose redemption.

I joined the Real Estate School, LLC part time while working full time. December 30th, 2024.

Eight days before I got my Clean Slate Expungement January 8th, 2025.

Time is of the essence! I started school January 6th, 2025 and graduated March 17, 2025.

Pardon to Patent

Usually it's the other way around! I'm happy to announce that I received my first patent during the release of this book!!!
Invention Title: NAVIGATION AND MONITORING SYSTEM CN Filing Date: March 05, 2025
CN Patent Application No.: 202530100754.3
Our Ref.: 03158RE03DES1US

Dear Colleagues,

We are pleased to report that we received the grant notification of the industrial design issued on October 10, 2025 by the China National Intellectual Property

Administration (CNIPA). The notification is attached for your reference.

The design is granted based on the documents submitted on March 05, 2025.

CHAPTER TEN:

GRIEF AND THE WEIGHT

OF LOSS

. . . .

People talk about grief like it has a timeline.

Like there's a point where the crying stops, the pain fades, and the world resets.

But grief don't own a clock.

It shows up when it wants, stays as long as it pleases, and leaves fingerprints all over your life.

If prison was the hardest place I ever survived, **grief was the heaviest thing I ever carried**.

Because unlike a sentence, grief doesn't have an end date.

You just learn how to walk with it—like a limp you never fully heal from.

The Losses Came in Waves

Even after I got out, even after I turned my life around, the losses never stopped.

It's like life kept testing my heart, asking, *"How much more can you take?"*

One of the deepest cuts came with the death of my **nephew Aaron. May 24, 2022**

Aaron was the same little boy who had been rescued off the roof during the fire. I remember the helicopter lifting him up like a fragile miracle that day.

He fought to live—and he did. For years. He grew into a man.

But life never got easy for him.

He got caught up in the system. Landed behind bars. And there, in prison custody—**just like me years earlier—he fell sick.**

They didn't listen.

They didn't care.

And by the time someone took it seriously…

it was too late.

He died from an infection at the same hospital where I had almost died.

The same place.

The same system.

The same silence.

It felt like déjà vu, but worse—because this time, we lost him for good.

My Niece Shadeequah May 11, 2023—Gone in Stillness

Not long after, we lost **Aaron's sister—my niece**.

She wasn't murdered. She wasn't in an accident. She was just... **found**.

Sitting on her couch. Gone.

The kind of quiet death that screams something's wrong.

I don't even have the words to describe what it feels like to get that call.

Because you think you've already cried all your tears.

You think your heart has already reached its limit.

But then God shows you there's **a deeper place** in your grief you haven't touched yet.

She left behind her daughter, **Blessing**. Blessing did at a very young age under five. My family and I helped put Shadeequah on the coroner's gurney. Blessing's name means something.

Because in the midst of all the loss, this child represents what's still possible.

She is the light left behind.

Aunt Estelle: The Backbone

When I lost **Aunt Estelle Phox August 4, 2020**, it felt like I lost my second mother.

After the fire, she opened her home to us. No hesitation. No questions. Just love and structure. Then her daughter Lisa passed away right after my Uncle David.

She had that **old-school kind of grace**—the kind that says, *"Get up, wipe your face, and let's move forward."* She gave us shelter, discipline, and the space to heal.

I didn't just admire her—I depended on her.

Losing her was like losing a part of my foundation.

The woman who caught me after the fire,

The woman who held the family together when it wanted to fall apart,

The woman who never asked for credit, but gave everything?

Gone.

Uncle David: Street Justice and Final Peace

Then came the loss of **Uncle David November 5, 2021**.

They used to whisper about him in the streets.

He was the one who allegedly **avenged the death of his brother Jesse**, a man who had been taken from us too soon.

Uncle David was part fighter, part philosopher.

He had seen the worst of the streets and made it out—but not without scars.

We talked often, but I felt his presence in everything I did.

He reminded me that family isn't perfect—but it's *ours*.

When he passed, I felt the flame dim a bit more.

More Names Than I Can List

I've lost **friends, cousins, old flames, neighbors, comrades** I served with, and **people I grew up playing hide-and-seek with** who ended up hiding from the world permanently —behind addictions, bitterness, or early graves.

Some were taken by **gunfire**.

Others by disease, despair, or disappearance.

The hood doesn't just bury bodies.

It buries potential, dreams, and whole generations if you let it.

What I Do With My Grief

I carry it. Every day.

But I don't let it make me bitter. I let it make me **better**.

I write.

I speak.

I build.

When I designed **Reyena**, I thought about Aaron. I thought about the kind of **witness** he didn't have when he was sick and ignored.

When I mentor young people, I think about my niece. About how easy it is to slip away without a word if nobody's checking on you.

When I hustle, when I dream, when I refuse to quit—I'm **doing it for them**.

Grief Is a Mirror

It shows you who you really are.

You either shrink or you stretch.

You either go numb or grow deeper.

You either fold or **you fight forward**.

I chose to fight.

Because every name I've lost along the way?

They're counting on me.

To finish the story.

To lift the family.

To carry the torch.

Grief didn't kill me.

It crowned me.

And now I walk with their names in my chest,

like rhythm in a drum, beating me forward.

CHAPTER ELEVEN
FULL CIRCLE - REAL
ESTATE AND RENEWED
PURPOSE

They say what goes around comes around.

But **full circle** ain't just about life repeating—it's about **life healing**.

It's about those rare moments where time, growth, pain, and faith meet in the middle and say: *"Now you understand."*

I've had a lot of circles in my life—circles of loss, circles of survival, circles of unfinished stories.

But in **2025**, I stepped into one I never saw coming.

On June 2nd, 2025—exactly **33 years to the day** after my niece **Diamond** was born right before I was released from Helene Fuld Hospital near death it changed my life forever…

…I passed the New Jersey State Real Estate Exam.

From Fire to Foundation

Let me take you back.

On **June 2nd, 1992**, while I was still recovering. Still displaced. Still emotionally shredded from the past losing **Shawn**, saving **Aaron**, and watching my life crumble.

That same year, **Diamond** was born.

Her birth was like a pulse returning to a flatlined body.

A sign that life goes on, even when you don't know how it can.

I watched her grow from a baby into a beautiful, fierce woman—through hard times, good times, and everything in between. And somewhere deep down, I promised myself: *"If I ever make it through all this, I'm going to show her what real recovery looks like."*

Fast forward 33 years—**same day**, different Hugh.

Different outcome.

I didn't just survive the fire.

I didn't just make it out of prison.

I didn't just beat the odds.

I became a licensed real estate professional in the State of New Jersey—after everything.

Why Real Estate?

Because I know what it's like to lose a home.

I know what it's like to **live out of bags**, sleep on couches, and pray you don't get evicted. I know what it's like to work hard and still **come up short on rent**. I know what it's like to rebuild from **literal ashes**.

So when I got the chance to study real estate, it wasn't just about income.

It was about **impact**.

I wanted to help people secure what I once lost:

Stability. Ownership. Safety.

Homes aren't just buildings. They're **sanctuaries**.

And I wanted to help people find theirs.

The Hustle Never Left Me

It wasn't easy. Studying while managing bills, rebuilding a business, and juggling health challenges wasn't a walk in the park. I had to **retrain my mind**, get back into student mode, and **block out distractions**.

But the same hustle that got me through the Army, through Excel Communications, through the development of Reyena—that hustle kicked in.

I studied late at night. Took notes like I was prepping for a war.

And when test day came, I didn't walk in with fear—I walked in with **purpose**.

I passed.

On the fifth try.

On Diamond's birthday. You can't make that up.

33 Years Later: Meaning in the Math

People who know me know I don't take signs lightly.

When I saw that date—June 2nd—it hit me like a whisper from God.

33 years after a baby girl was born in the shadow of tragedy, her uncle stood tall, fully licensed, fully pardoned, fully transformed.

It was more than poetic. It was **divine math**.

One life began in crisis.

Another was reborn in triumph—same day, same bloodline, same spirit.

Now It's Bigger Than Me

Real estate is just a license on paper.

But what I do with it? That's legacy. I want to teach financial literacy, I want to help single mothers, returning citizens, veterans, and young dreamers find stability.

I want to show them that no matter where you start, no matter what flames you walk through—**you can own your future.**

And I want to do it all with **Reyena** still in development, with music still playing in the background, with my family's names stitched into every move I make.

From Trauma to Title Deeds

That's the full circle.

That's what healing looks like.

Not perfection—but progress.

From being homeless to helping others find homes.

From being incarcerated to licensed.

From being written off to being the writer of my own story.

That's what this chapter is.

Not just about real estate.

But about reclaiming everything that once felt out of reach.

I didn't just pass a test.

I honored my past.

And I showed my future that I'm not done building yet.On December 20, 2024, I received the official copy of my executive pardon.

Ten days later, on December 30, 2024, I signed up for The Real Estate School. There was no time to celebrate—not yet. That could wait. I had my eyes on the future and was determined to seize this second chance at building something better for myself. That $545 I spent on the real estate course? It felt like the most gratifying investment I'd made in a long time—an investment not just in a career, but in the man I was finally becoming.

It took me back to 1974, sitting in front of my junior high school guidance counselor.

Like she did with every student, she asked me what I wanted to be when I grew up. I told her, straight up, either a lawyer or a doctor.

At this stage in life, real estate might be the closest I'll get to either one of those professions, and you know what? I'm humble, and I'm grateful. Within six months of receiving my full executive pardon and Clean Slate expungement, I was already paving a new road forward.

I knew that if I had allowed myself to start celebrating too soon, I might've lost that focus. And I couldn't afford that— not now. Not with the clock ticking on opportunity. I had to stay in motion, keep my momentum.

One thing I've learned is: never say what you ain't goin' to do. It just might happen. That reminds me of the scripture: *"As a man thinketh in his heart, so is he."* I've made that mistake—for you—so you don't have to.

CHAPTER TWELVE:

FAMILY LEGACY FROM
THE SHOULDERS OF A
GIANT

. . . .

The year 2009 took a heavy toll on our family. That was the year I lost my youngest brother, **Kevin Brian Harris**—a man whose presence in our lives was both grounding and inspiring. He was one of those quiet giants who carried the weight of generations on his shoulders without ever asking for anything in return.

He left behind not just memories, but a legacy in the form of his two sons: **Apostle Everton Wayne Harris** and **Kevin Michael Harris**.

Kevin's passing left a wound, but his legacy lives on in the strength, purpose, and faith of his children. As the oldest, **Apostle Everton Wayne Harris** stepped into manhood with a heart for service and a calling that couldn't be ignored.

I had the honor of being the videographer at his wedding to his beautiful wife **Corinthia**—a sacred moment that bonded not only two hearts, but two legacies together.

From early on, Everton felt drawn to serve others, especially the youth. He found a path in ministry, becoming both a youth minister and later a pastor, dedicating himself to shaping the minds and spirits of young people searching for meaning. At one point, Everton was working closely with **Greg Grant**, another product of Trenton's struggle and spirit.

Grant, who had grown up in a broken home himself, worked in a fish market during high school. But his hustle didn't go unnoticed.

Discovered at a local playground, Grant defied odds. Standing only 5-foot-7, he still managed to lead Division III basketball in scoring during his time at Trenton State College— now known as **The College of New Jersey (TCNJ)**. In 1989, his grind paid off when the **Phoenix Suns** selected him 52nd overall in the NBA draft. He went on to play six seasons in the NBA for six different teams, proving that passion and grit could overcome size and circumstance. After retiring, he came back to Trenton and founded the **Greg Grant Sports Academy**, where he taught kids the same values that shaped his journey: discipline, faith, and perseverance.

Everton brought those same values to the court and the pulpit. He coached and mentored kids at the academy with passion, loving them like they were his own. But as life often goes, doors that seem sturdy can suddenly close. He was let go from his position at the academy—a gut punch that could've broken a lesser man. But Everton? He never lost faith.

I remember telling him during one of our conversations, "When one door closes, another one opens—but not just any door. The door God opens will be the one that fits the key you already hold in your heart."

That key was Jesus. And true to the faith he lived by, Everton didn't just move on—he leveled up.

He and Corinthia relocated to **Raleigh, North Carolina**, where they planted new roots. There, they founded the **Divine Restoration Worship Center**, a ministry born from experience, hardship, and the belief that transformation is possible for anyone. Their faith was not just spoken—it was lived out daily. Together, they are raising **three beautiful children**, nurturing a new generation grounded in love, leadership, and purpose.

But they didn't stop at church walls. Their vision expanded to education. They began working on their next dream: a school called **Divine Scholars Preparatory Academy**—a place where kids could learn not only academics but also the values of restoration, discipline, and divine purpose. That's legacy building. That's what standing on the shoulders of a giant looks like.

As for Kevin's namesake—**Kevin Michael Harris**—he carved his own path with a steady stride. He graduated from **Rutgers University**, earning a degree in **Sports Management**, blending academic achievement with a passion for athletics that surely ran in the bloodline. He may not always be in the spotlight, but his journey shows that legacy doesn't need a microphone to make noise. Sometimes it speaks softly through resilience and quiet determination.

So here we are. A family shaped by loss, but defined by resilience. Kevin Brian Harris may no longer walk among us, but every step his sons take—every sermon preached, every youth coached, every child taught—echoes the greatness of the man who raised them.

From the shoulders of a giant, new giants are being born. That's why I feel it's imperative that I highlight my nephew Bishop Everton Wayne Harris Sr. and his wife Corinthia Harris in their journey to continue to help the youth with this new academy.

DIVINE SCHOLARS PREPARATORY ACADEMY

"NURTURING BRILLIANCE, EMPOWERING FUTURES"

Divine Scholars Preparatory Academy Executive Summary

Divine Scholars Preparatory Academy is an innovative educational institution that offers a comprehensive curriculum, integrating STEM (Science, Technology, Engineering, and Mathematics) and Business classes. By offering educational experience that equips students with the knowledge, skills, and mindset necessary to thrive in an ever-evolving world. By combining STEM education with comprehensive Business classes, we prepare students innovative problem solvers, ethical leader, and contributors to society.

Our mission is to provide a transformative learning experience that prepares students for the dynamic and interconnected world of the 21st century.

Key Points:

- Holistic Education: Divine Scholars Preparatory Academy offers a holistic approach to education, focusing on the development of academic excellence, critical thinking, creativity, and problem-solving skills. Through our STEM and Business classes, we equip students with a well-rounded foundation that prepares them for future success.

- STEM Education: We prioritize STEM education to foster a deep understanding of scientific principles, technological advancements, and engineering design. Our students engage in hands-on experiments, projects, and coding activities, nurturing their curiosity and empowering them to become innovative thinkers and problem solvers.

- Business Classes: Divine Scholars Preparatory Academy recognizes the importance of business education in the modern world. We provide comprehensive Business classes that introduce students to entrepreneurship, marketing, financial literacy, and ethical business practices. Through real-world simulations and hands-on experiences, our students develop essential skills for success in the business realm.

- Integrated Curriculum: Our curriculum seamlessly integrates STEM and Business classes with other core subjects, promoting cross-disciplinary learning and application. This approach allows students to make connections between various disciplines, fostering a holistic understanding of how knowledge is interconnected and applicable to real world situations.

- Experienced Faculty: At Divine Scholars Preparatory Academy, we pride ourselves on our experienced and passionate faculty. Our educators bring expertise in STEM fields and business entrepreneurship, ensuring that students receive high-quality instruction and mentorship. They are committed to nurturing each student's individual talents and providing a supportive learning environment. Goals:

- Foster Critical Thinking: Our primary goal is to foster critical thinking skills in students through problem-solving activities, analytical reasoning, and experimentation. We encourage students to ask questions, challenge assumptions, and think of innovation.

- Develop Technological Competence: Divine Scholars Preparatory Academy aims to develop students' technological competence by providing them with the necessary skills to thrive in a technology-driven world. Through coding, robotics, and digital literacy, we empower students to become confident users and creators of technology.

- Nurture Entrepreneurial Mindset: We strive to instill an entrepreneurial mindset in our students, encouraging them to identify opportunities, take calculated risks, and develop creative solutions. By fostering an environment that supports innovation and business acumen, we prepare students for future success in entrepreneurial endeavors.

• Promote Collaboration and Communication: Divine Scholars Preparatory Academy emphasizes the importance of collaboration and effective communication skills. We provide opportunities for teamwork, presentations, and group projects, enabling students to collaborate, share ideas, and express themselves confidently.

Cultivate Ethical Leadership: Our goal is to cultivate ethical leaders who understand the importance of integrity, social responsibility, and ethical decision- making. Through our business classes, we foster an understanding of ethical business practices, encouraging students to become responsible leaders in their future careers.

Our Purpose:

Our purpose of Divine Scholars Preparatory Academy is to empower students with a comprehensive education that integrates STEM (Science, Technology, Engineering, and Mathematics) principles and cultivates a strong foundation in business entrepreneurship.

Our Mission:

Our mission is to foster a dynamic learning environment that nurtures curiosity, critical thinking, creativity, and collaboration, equipping students with the skills, knowledge, and mindset to excel in an ever-evolving global society. Through rigorous academic programs, hands-on experiences, and real-world applications, we aim to inspire students to become innovative problem solvers, ethical leaders, and lifelong learners, prepared to make meaningful contributions to the fields of STEM and business entrepreneurship, and positively impact their communities and beyond.

Our Vision:

Our vision of Divine Scholars Preparatory Academy is to be a beacon of educational excellence, innovation, and empowerment, where students thrive in a dynamic and inclusive learning community. We envision a future where our students embrace the limitless possibilities of STEM (Science, Technology, Engineering, and Mathematics) and business entrepreneurship, becoming trailblazers and change-makers in their respective fields.

At Divine Scholars Preparatory Academy, we aspire to cultivate a passion for discovery and a deep understanding of STEM principles, enabling our students to unlock their full potential as critical thinkers, problem solvers, and inventors. Through hands-on experiences, cutting-edge technologies, and collaborative projects, our students will develop the skills and mindset necessary to tackle complex challenges, push boundaries, and drive transformative advancements in science, technology, engineering, and mathematics.

In parallel, we envision Divine Scholars Preparatory Academy as a cradle of business entrepreneurship, fostering a culture of innovation, resilience, and ethical leadership. Our students will be empowered with the knowledge, skills, and mindset required to navigate the ever-changing business landscape, develop sustainable ventures, and make meaningful contributions to economic growth and social progress.

By integrating STEM and business entrepreneurship, we envision Divine Scholars

Preparatory Academy as a hub of interdisciplinary exploration, where students embrace

the interconnections between science, technology, engineering, mathematics, and

business, unlocking a realm of boundless opportunities. We strive to nurture a

supportive and inclusive environment that celebrates diversity, collaboration, and

creativity, preparing our students to thrive in a globally connected world.

Ultimately, our vision is to inspire and empower the future generation of STEM leaders

and business entrepreneurs who will shape a brighter future, solve pressing societal

challenges, and forge new paths of innovation, progress, and positive change in their

communities and beyond

Our Core Values:

Our core values at Divine Scholars Preparatory Academy are:

1. Excellence: We strive for excellence in all aspects of education, fostering a culture of high standards, rigorous learning, and continuous improvement. We instill in our students a commitment to achieving their personal best in STEM and business entrepreneurship, setting the stage for future success.

2. Innovation: We embrace innovation as a driving force in STEM and business entrepreneurship. We encourage creative thinking, problem-solving, and the exploration of new ideas, technologies, and methodologies. Our students develop a mindset of adaptability and resilience, embracing challenges as opportunities for growth and innovation.

3. Collaboration: We foster a collaborative and inclusive community where teamwork, cooperation, and respect are valued. We believe that diverse perspectives enrich the learning experience and contribute to innovative solutions. Our students learn to collaborate effectively, understanding the power of collective intelligence in advancing STEM and business entrepreneurship.

4.   Ethical Leadership: We emphasize the importance of ethical conduct, integrity, and responsible decision-making. Our students develop strong moral values, guided by a sense of social responsibility and a commitment to ethical practices in STEM and business entrepreneurship. They are equipped with the skills to lead with integrity and make ethical choices that positively impact their communities.

5.   Real-World Relevance: We prioritize real-world application of knowledge and skills in STEM and business entrepreneurship. Our curriculum integrates practical experiences, project-based learning, and experiential opportunities that bridge classroom learning with authentic, hands-on experiences. This approach prepares our students to apply their knowledge and skills to real-world challenges and equips them for success in their future endeavors.

6.   Lifelong Learning: We foster a love for learning and a growth mindset in our students. We encourage them to be lifelong learners, constantly seeking new knowledge, refining their skills, and adapting to a rapidly changing world. Our students develop a curiosity-driven approach to STEM and business entrepreneurship, embracing continuous learning and personal growth throughout their lives.

By upholding these core values, Divine Scholars Preparatory Academy aims to nurture a generation of well-rounded individuals who are not only proficient in STEM and business entrepreneurship but also demonstrate integrity, resilience, and a commitment to making a positive impact in the world.

Background and Rationale

Divine Scholars Preparatory Academy was established to address the evolving needs of the 21st-Century educational landscape. Our aim is to provide a forward-thinking educational institution that combines STEM (

Identifying Gaps in the Existing Educational System:

- Lack of Emphasis on STEM Education: Traditional educational systems often fail to provide sufficient focus on STEM subjects, despite the growing importance of these fields in shaping our world. There is a need for educational institutions that prioritize STEM education to equip students with the necessary skills for success in today's highly competitive job market.

- Limited Exposure to Business Concepts: Many schools do not offer comprehensive Business classes, leaving students ill-prepared to navigate the complexities of the business world. There is a need to bridge this gap by providing students with a solid foundation in entrepreneurship, marketing, financial literacy, and ethical business practices.

- Integration of STEM and Business: While some schools may offer STEM

or Business classes separately, there is a lack of integration between these disciplines. Divine Scholars Academy recognizes the value of integrating STEM and Business education to foster interdisciplinary thinking, problem-solving, and innovation.

Supporting Research and Data:

- Growing Demand for STEM Skills: According to the U.S. Bureau of Labor Statistics, occupations in STEM fields are projected to grow at a faster rate than non-STEM occupations. This highlights the importance of equipping students with STEM skills to meet future workforce demands.

- Importance of Business Education: Research by organizations such as the National Association for College Admission Counseling (NACAC) and the Association for Career and Technical Education (ACTE) underscores the

Science, Technology, Engineering, and

Mathematics) and Business classes, catering to the demands of an increasingly

interconnected and technologically driven world.

significance of business education in preparing students for career success and entrepreneurship opportunities.

c. Interdisciplinary Approach: Studies have shown that an interdisciplinary approach to education, integrating STEM and Business subjects, enhances students' critical thinking, problem-solving, and collaboration skills. This approach prepares them to tackle real-world challenges that require a multifaceted understanding of complex issues.

d. Long-Term Impact: Research indicates that early exposure to STEM and business concepts can positively influence students' career aspirations and academic performance. It helps foster a mindset of innovation, entrepreneurship, and lifelong learning.

In light of these gaps and research findings, Divine Scholars Preparatory Academy was established to provide a comprehensive education that combines STEM and Business classes. By integrating these disciplines, we aim to create a learning environment that nurtures critical thinking, innovation, collaboration, and ethical leadership. Our approach aligns with the demands of the modern workforce and empowers students to become well-rounded individuals capable of making meaningful contributions to their communities and beyond.

Through Divine Scholars Preparatory Academy, students will gain a strong foundation in STEM subjects, develop technological competence, and cultivate an entrepreneurial mindset. They will also be equipped with essential business knowledge, ethical principles, and leadership skills. By addressing these gaps in the existing educational system, Divine Scholars Preparatory Academy aims to prepare students for a future where STEM and business concepts intersect, fostering their success in a rapidly changing world.

Our Philosophy and Learning Model

At Divine Scholars Preparatory Academy, we believe in empowering our students to excel in the fields of Science, Technology, Engineering, and Mathematics (STEM), while also fostering their entrepreneurial spirit. Our philosophy revolves around providing a comprehensive education that combines rigorous academic training with practical skills, critical thinking, and ethical values. We strive to create an environment that nurtures innovation, creativity, and a passion for problem-solving, preparing our students to become future leaders and change makers in the STEM and business sectors.

By embracing this philosophy and learning model, Divine Scholars Preparatory Academy equips students with the knowledge, skills, and mindset required to thrive in the dynamic and competitive fields of STEM and business entrepreneurship. We aim to nurture a new generation of innovators, problem-solvers, and ethical leaders who can drive positive change and contribute to the advancement of society in meaningful and sustainable ways.

Learning Model:

1. STEM Integration: We offer a curriculum that seamlessly integrates STEM subjects into various disciplines, encouraging students to explore the intersections between science, technology, engineering, mathematics, and other fields such as business, arts, and social sciences. This interdisciplinary approach enables students to develop a comprehensive understanding of how STEM knowledge can be applied in real-world contexts.

2. Hands-on Learning: We emphasize experiential and project-based learning, providing students with opportunities to engage in hands-on activities, experiments, and design projects. By applying theoretical concepts to practical scenarios, students develop problem-solving skills, critical thinking abilities, and a deep understanding of the scientific and entrepreneurial processes.

3. Entrepreneurship Education: We incorporate entrepreneurship education into our curriculum, enabling students to cultivate an entrepreneurial mindset and develop business acumen. Students learn about market analysis, product development, financial management, marketing strategies, and business ethics. They are encouraged to generate innovative ideas, create business plans, and collaborate on entrepreneurial projects.

4. Industry Partnerships: We establish partnerships with local businesses, startups, research institutions, and industry experts to provide students with real-world exposure and mentorship opportunities. Through internships, guest lectures, and industry visits, students gain valuable insights into the STEM and business sectors, developing a network of professional contacts and fostering an entrepreneurial mindset.

5. Technology Integration: We embrace the latest technologies and tools to enhance the learning experience. Students have access to state-of-the-art laboratories, computer programming software, 3D printers, robotics kits, and other resources. They are encouraged to explore emerging technologies, develop digital literacy, and leverage technology to solve complex problems and drive innovation.

6. Ethical Leadership: We emphasize the importance of ethical leadership and responsible decision-making in STEM and business fields. Students engage in

discussions and case studies that address ethical dilemmas, corporate social responsibility, and sustainability. They are encouraged to consider the societal and environmental impacts of their work, nurturing a sense of responsibility towards the greater good.

7. Collaboration and Teamwork: We foster a collaborative learning environment where students engage in teamwork, communication, and problem-solving with their peers. Through group projects, debates, and simulations, students develop interpersonal skills, learn from diverse perspectives, and cultivate the ability to work effectively in teams—an essential skill in STEM and entrepreneurial endeavors.

8. Growth Mindset and Resilience: We instill in our students a growth mindset, emphasizing the importance of perseverance, resilience, and embracing failure as an opportunity for learning and growth. Students are encouraged to take risks, learn from setbacks, and develop the resilience needed to overcome challenges in their STEM and entrepreneurial pursuits.

Target Market and Demographics

Divine Scholars Preparatory Academy aims to cater to a diverse range of students who will benefit from our unique educational approach that integrates STEM (Science, Technology, Engineering, and Mathematics) and Business classes.

Our target market encompasses:

• Age Range: Divine Scholars Preparatory Academy welcomes students from Pre- K to 12th grade. Our comprehensive curriculum is designed to provide a seamless educational journey from early childhood to high school graduation, allowing students to experience the benefits of our integrated STEM and Business programs throughout their academic years.

• Geographical Location: Divine Scholars Preparatory Academy is situated in a vibrant and accessible location that serves families from both urban and suburban areas. Our goal is to be conveniently located to ensure easy access for students and their families, creating a welcoming and inclusive community.

• Demographics:
a. All Students: Divine Scholars Preparatory Academy is open to students from all backgrounds, irrespective of gender, race, ethnicity, or socioeconomic status. We believe in creating a diverse and inclusive learning environment where students can interact and learn from one another's perspectives.

b. Special Needs Students: Divine Scholars Preparatory Academy is committed to inclusivity and providing support for students with diverse learning needs. Our goal is to offer an inclusive environment that accommodates the unique requirements of students with disabilities, ensuring they receive the necessary resources and support to thrive academically and personally.

c. Gifted and Talented Students: Divine Scholars Preparatory Academy recognizes the importance of meeting the needs of gifted and talented students. We provide enrichment opportunities, advanced coursework, and specialized programs to challenge and inspire these students, nurturing their exceptional abilities and helping them reach their full potential.

By catering to a diverse range of students, including special needs students and gifted students, Divine Scholars Preparatory Academy seeks to create an inclusive and enriching educational experience that supports the unique needs and talents of each student. We celebrate diversity and foster an environment where all students can thrive, learn from one another, and develop the necessary skills for success in the fields of STEM and business entrepreneurship.

Grade Level Curriculum Early Childhood Scholars Pre-K and Kindergarten

Pre-K to Kindergarten, incorporating STEM (Science, Technology, Engineering, and Mathematics) concepts. This curriculum focuses on hands-on, experiential learning, promoting curiosity, exploration, and problem-solving skills in young learners. Throughout Pre-K and Kindergarten, it is important to incorporate cross-curricular activities that integrate STEM concepts with other subjects such as language arts, art, and social studies. Additionally, hands-on experiments, field trips, and guest speakers can enhance students' understanding of STEM topics and their applications in the real world. It's essential to foster a supportive and inquiry-based learning environment where students can explore, ask questions, and engage in problem-solving activities.

Pre-K:

1. Mathematics:
o Number recognition and counting
o Sorting and classifying objects
o Introduction to shapes and patterns

2. Science:
o Exploring the five senses
o Observing and describing changes in the environment

o Basic concepts of living and non-living things 3. Technology:

o Introduction to simple technological tools (e.g., tablets, interactive boards) o Educational apps and games for early learning
o Basic computer skills (mouse, keyboard)

4. Engineering:
o Building with blocks and construction materials o Simple problem-solving activities and challenges o Introduction to cause-and-effect relationships

Kindergarten:

1. Mathematics:
o Number sense and place value
o Addition and subtraction within
o Introduction to measurement and basic geometry

2. Science:
o Exploring weather and seasons
o Introduction to plants and animals
o Hands-on experiments and observations

3. Technology:
o Basic computer skills and digital literacy
o Introduction to coding concepts through interactive games o Digital storytelling and multimedia presentations

4. Engineering:

o Building structures with various materials
o Introduction to simple machines and their functions o
Engaging in engineering design challenges

Primary School Scholars Students $1^{st} - 5^{th}$

This curriculum is designed to provide an introduction to both STEM and entrepreneurship while fostering creativity, critical thinking, problem-solving, and business skills. The curriculum can be adapted based on the specific resources, interests, and needs of the students and school. Additionally, incorporating guest speakers, field trips, and real-world connections can further enhance the learning experience.

1st Grade:

1. Mathematics:

o Number recognition and counting
o Basic addition and subtraction
o Introduction to shapes and patterns

2. Science:

o Introduction to the scientific method
o Exploring the five senses
o Basic concepts of living and non-living things

3. Technology:
o Basic computer skills (mouse, keyboard, operating systems) o Introduction to coding concepts through interactive games

4. Engineering:
o Building structures with blocks and other materials
o Introduction to simple machines (levers, pulleys, etc.)

5. Business:
o Basic understanding of money and currency o Introduction to needs vs. wants
o Exploring different jobs and careers

2nd Grade:

1. Mathematics:
o Place value and number sense
o Addition and subtraction strategies
o Introduction to basic multiplication and division

2. Science:
o Exploring plants and animals
o Introduction to weather and seasons
o Conducting simple experiments and recording observations

3. Technology:

o Introduction to word processing and typing skills o Basic internet safety and digital citizenship

4. Engineering:

o Design and build simple bridges and towers
o Introduction to robotics and programming concepts

5. Business:

o Introduction to entrepreneurship
o Identifying goods and services
o Basic financial literacy and budgeting

3rd Grade:

1. Mathematics:

o Multiplication and division facts
o Introduction to fractions and decimals o Measurement and data analysis

2. Science:

o States of matter and changes
o Introduction to energy and forces
o Exploration of ecosystems and habitats

3. Technology:

o Introduction to presentation software

o Digital research skills and online resources 4. Engineering:

o Design and build simple circuits

o Introduction to engineering design process and problem-solving 5. Business:

o Understanding supply and demand
o Introduction to marketing and advertising
o Basic entrepreneurship skills and business plans

4th Grade:

1. Mathematics:
o Multiplication and division of larger numbers o Introduction to geometry and angles
o Data analysis and probability

2. Science:
o Earth and space exploration
o Introduction to the human body and health o Basic concepts of matter and energy

3. Technology:

o Introduction to spreadsheets and data manipulation o Coding concepts and block-based programming

4. Engineering:

o Introduction to structural engineering and stability
o Design and build simple machines and mechanisms

5. Business:

o Introduction to economic systems
o Basics of personal finance and budgeting o Introduction to global markets and trade

5th Grade:

1. Mathematics:

o Fractions, decimals, and percentages
o Introduction to algebraic thinking
o Geometric concepts and measurements

2. Science:

o Introduction to scientific inquiry and experimentation o Exploration of environmental science
o Introduction to chemistry and the periodic table

3. Technology:

o Introduction to multimedia presentations and design
o Coding concepts and transitioning to text-based programming

4. Engineering:

o Design and build structures for specific purposes

o Introduction to automation and robotics 5. Business:

o Introduction to business ethics and social responsibility
o Market research and consumer behavior
o Basics of project management and teamwork

Intermediate Scholars Middle School Curriculum 6th – 8th

The curriculum for 6th grade to 8th grade, incorporating STEM (Science, Technology, Engineering, and Mathematics) and Business classes. This curriculum builds upon the foundation laid in the earlier grades and introduces more advanced concepts and skills. In addition to these subjects, it's important to incorporate practical hands-on activities, project-based learning, and real-world applications throughout the curriculum. This approach will help students develop critical thinking, problem-solving, collaboration, and creativity skills, which are essential in both STEM and business fields.

6th Grade:

1. Mathematics:

o Review of fundamental math concepts
o Introduction to ratios, proportions, and percentages o Basic algebraic expressions and equations

2. Science:

o Introduction to scientific method and inquiry
o Earth science (geology, weather, and climate) o Life science (cells, genetics, and biodiversity)

3. Technology:

o Digital literacy and online research skills
o Introduction to coding languages (Python, Scratch) o Multimedia design and presentation skills

4. Engineering:

o Introduction to engineering design principles
o Building and testing simple machines and mechanisms o Basic programming concepts for robotics

5. Business:

o Foundations of business and economics
o Introduction to market research and analysis o Basics of personal finance and budgeting

7th Grade:

1. Mathematics:

o Advanced algebraic concepts (linear equations, inequalities) o Geometry and spatial reasoning
o Data analysis and probability

2. Science:
o Physical science (matter, energy, and forces) o Introduction to chemistry and periodic table
o Scientific experimentation and data analysis

3. Technology:
o Intermediate coding and programming skills
o Web design and development basics
o Introduction to cybersecurity and online safety

4. Engineering:
o Advanced engineering design projects o Electronics and circuitry
o Introduction to 3D modeling and printing

5. Business:
o Entrepreneurship and business planning
o Marketing strategies and promotion
o Introduction to business ethics and social responsibility

8th Grade:

1. Mathematics:

o Advanced algebra and functions
o Geometric concepts (angles, congruence, similarity) o Introduction to statistics and probability

2. Science:

o Life science (ecology, human body, and health) o Introduction to physics and energy
o Environmental science and sustainability

3. Technology:

o Advanced coding and programming concepts
o Data analysis and visualization
o Introduction to artificial intelligence and machine learning

4. Engineering:

o Complex engineering design challenges o Robotics and automation projects
o Introduction to aerospace engineering

5. Business:

o Financial literacy and investing

o Business management and leadership skills
o Entrepreneurship projects and business simulations

Secondary School Scholars High School $9^{th} - 12^{th}$ Curriculum

This curriculum for the 9th grade to 12th grade, incorporating STEM (Science, Technology, Engineering, and Mathematics) and Business classes. This curriculum is designed to provide students with a comprehensive education in STEM and business fields, preparing them for higher education or careers in these areas. Throughout high school, it's crucial to provide opportunities for interdisciplinary projects, research experiences, and collaboration with industry professionals. Additionally, students should have access to extracurricular activities, competitions, and mentorship programs related to STEM and business fields. These experiences will enhance their knowledge, skills, and real-world applications of the subjects they study.

9th Grade:

1. Mathematics:
o Algebra II and advanced algebraic concepts o Geometry and trigonometry
o Introduction to calculus or pre-calculus

5. Science:
o Physics (mechanics, energy, and waves)
o Chemistry (atomic structure, chemical reactions) o Scientific inquiry and research methods

3. Technology:

o Advanced programming and software development o Web development and application design

o Introduction to databases and data management

6. Engineering:

o Engineering principles and problem-solving

o Robotics and automation projects

o Introduction to engineering disciplines (civil, mechanical, electrical, etc.)

5. Business:

o Business fundamentals and principles

o Marketing and consumer behavior

o Introduction to business communications and presentations

10th Grade:

1. Mathematics:

o Advanced calculus or statistics

o Mathematical modeling and problem-solving

o Financial mathematics and applications 2. Science:

o Biology (cellular biology, genetics, and evolution)
o Environmental science and sustainability
o Advanced laboratory techniques and experimentation

3. Technology:
o Advanced coding languages and algorithms o Data analysis and visualization
o Cybersecurity and ethical hacking

4. Engineering:
o Advanced engineering design projects and challenges o Systems engineering and integration
o Emerging technologies and their applications

5. Business:
o Financial accounting and analysis
o Entrepreneurship and business planning
o Business ethics and corporate social responsibility

11th Grade:

1. Mathematics:
o Advanced calculus or statistics (AP level) o Applied mathematics and modeling
o Mathematical reasoning and proofs

2. Science:

o Advanced topics in physics, chemistry, or biology (AP level) o Research methodologies and experimental design
o Introduction to scientific writing and publication

3. Technology:

o Advanced topics in computer science and software engineering (AP level) o Artificial intelligence and machine learning
o Internet of Things (IoT) and data-driven technologies

4. Engineering:

o Specialized engineering tracks (e.g., aerospace, biomedical,

environmental)
o Engineering research projects and internships o Professional engineering practices and ethics

5. Business:

o Business management and leadership skills
o International business and global markets
o Advanced business simulations and case studies

12th Grade:

1. Mathematics:
o Advanced topics in calculus, statistics, or discrete mathematics (AP level) o Mathematics in real-world contexts
o College-level mathematics courses (if available)

2. Science:
o College-level science courses (e.g., AP Biology, AP Chemistry, AP

Physics)
o Independent research projects in a scientific discipline o Science seminars and presentations

3. Technology:
o Advanced topics in computer science and emerging technologies o Mobile app development and software engineering projects
o Capstone projects showcasing technological innovation

4. Engineering:
o Engineering design and innovation projects
o Engineering internships or cooperative education programs
o Preparation for professional engineering licensure (if desired)

5. Business:
o Advanced business courses (e.g., economics, finance, marketing) o Business internships or entrepreneurship experiences
o Business plan development and presentation

Facilities and Resources

Divine Scholars Preparatory Academy recognizes the crucial role of well-designed facilities and resources in providing a dynamic and immersive learning environment that integrates STEM (Science, Technology, Engineering, and Mathematics) and Business classes.

Our commitment to excellence in education is supported by the following infrastructure:

• Classrooms: We prioritize modern and flexible classrooms that promote collaboration and active learning. Each classroom is equipped with interactive whiteboards, audiovisual systems, and ergonomic furniture. The learning spaces are designed to accommodate various teaching methods and foster student engagement.

• STEM Laboratories: Divine Scholars Preparatory Academy places a strong emphasis on practical, hands-on learning in STEM fields. We provide fully equipped laboratories for biology, chemistry, physics, and engineering. These state-of-the-art facilities allow students to conduct experiments, engage in research projects, and apply theoretical concepts to real-world scenarios.

- Business Incubator: To support the Business classes, Divine Scholars Preparatory Academy offers a dedicated business incubator space. This innovative facility provides students with a simulated entrepreneurial environment, equipped with business software, collaboration areas, and presentation spaces. It serves as a hub for students to develop and implement business ideas, engage in group projects, and learn from experienced mentors.

- Library and Resource Center: Our school features a comprehensive library and resource center that serves as a hub of knowledge and exploration. The library houses a vast collection of books, e-books, journals, and online resources related to STEM, business, and other academic disciplines. It also provides quiet study areas, research support, and technology resources for students' academic pursuits.

- Sports and Fitness Facilities: Divine Scholars Preparatory Academy recognizes the importance of physical fitness and well-being in the holistic development of students. We provide well-maintained sports facilities, including a gymnasium, outdoor fields, and courts. These spaces enable students to participate in various sports activities, promoting teamwork, discipline, and a healthy lifestyle.

- Technology Resources: We ensure that our school is equipped with up-to-date technology resources to support digital learning and innovation. This includes computer labs, laptops, tablets, and multimedia equipment. Our network infrastructure supports robust internet connectivity, allowing students and teachers to utilize online resources, collaborate on projects, and engage in virtual learning experiences.

CHAPTER THIRTEEN:
THE RECOLLECTION OF MY COLLECTION

Some people remember their lives through photographs. Others keep journals or home movies. Me? I remember mine through the sound of the needle dropping on wax.

I was just **eight years old** when I bought my first 45. It was **"The Love You Save" by the Jackson 5**, and I played it until the grooves ran smooth.

That record became my first time capsule. Little did I know, it would be the start of a collection that would come to represent not just my personal taste, but a living history of an era —**a soundtrack to survival**.

Growing up, we didn't have much. But in our house, **music was everything**. The floor-model record player stood like a monument in our living room. Its wood finish gleamed under the light, and when you lifted the top, it revealed a turntable and radio—a two-in-one command center of joy.

The built-in speakers filled every corner of our apartment with soul, funk, and messages of love, heartbreak, and resilience. That stereo was my altar. Those songs were my sermons.

When the fire came years later—ripping through life, memories, and material things—so much was lost. And yet somehow, **my 45s survived**. Melted plastic, charred edges, the smell of smoke still clinging to the sleeves… but they were still there. **They made it**, just like I did. Each record a survivor. Each label, a memory. Each spin, a miracle.

That collection is a **musical memoir**—a testimony of life before and after the fire. Some people collect stamps, coins, or baseball cards. I collected moments. Moments you could dance to. Moments you could cry to. Moments you fell in love, or out of it.

There was **Gladys Knight & The Pips** reminding us that "On and On," life doesn't stop for sorrow. There was the **Stylistics** laying down the truth with "Break Up to Make Up" and "Stone in Love with You." **Al Green** told me to love deeper. **The Bar-Kays** told me to party harder. And **Stevie Wonder**—he always took me to a higher place, especially with "Saturn" and "All Day Sucker."

Some songs were funky escapes—like **"Jungle Boogie" by Kool & The Gang** or **"Boogie Oogie Oogie" by A Taste of Honey**—they let you lose yourself in rhythm. Others like **"Woman to Woman" by Shirley Brown** or **"Me and Mrs. Jones" by Billy Paul** cracked open real stories about betrayal and desire that even a kid didn't fully understand but still felt deep down.

And of course, the **quiet storm anthems**: **The Manhattans' "Kiss and Say Goodbye"**, **Heatwave's "Always and Forever,"** and **Teddy Pendergrass' "Close the Door."** Those joints raised us. Taught us how to talk smooth, how to apologize, how to romance. You didn't need a therapist—you needed **Donny Hathaway and Roberta Flack** telling you how "The Closer I Get to You" could save a broken moment.

The collection kept growing—**over 140 45s** that painted the full spectrum of love, funk, disco, heartbreak, redemption, and real life.

Artists like **Maze, The Gap Band, Earth, Wind & Fire, Deniece Williams, Chaka Khan, KC and the Sunshine Band**, and so many others filled the crate with stories I could feel deep in my soul. **Music wasn't just a sound—it was a sanctuary.**

Looking back, those records weren't just entertainment. They were **preservation**—of joy, of struggle, of Black excellence, of a cultural renaissance that happened in the basements, block parties, and bedrooms of the 1970s and early 1980s. Before the algorithms, before the playlists, we made our own mixes by flipping the record over and dancing until the needle lifted itself.

I think about how those songs helped me survive every stage of life—through my parents' separation, heartbreak, prison, my nephew Shawn's tragic loss, the ups and downs of relationships, and even my executive pardon. **Every trial had a soundtrack. Every comeback had a beat.**

I can still hear **"Be Thankful for What You Got"** by William DeVaughn playing while I sat in my room, dreaming of a better future. I still remember the chills from **Luther Ingram's "(If Loving You Is Wrong) I Don't Want to Be Right"**, and how **The O'Jays** reminded me of heartbreak's edge with "Use Ta Be My Girl."

And now, as I write this chapter—the final one in this journey—I can't help but smile. That old floor model record player may be long gone. But the music? It's still spinning in my heart.

This collection survived the flames so I could tell this story. It's more than vinyl and grooves. It's a record of who I was, who I became, and how I made it through.

The collection is me.

And I am still playing.

EPILOGUE: RESILIENCE, RESTORATION, AND THE RHYTHM OF REDEMPTION

I didn't write this book to glorify my past. I wrote it to testify to what's possible when **you don't give up**—even when you've been knocked down, locked out, or written off.

This is more than just a personal story—it's a **blueprint** for transformation. From a childhood marked by instability to a man haunted by mistakes, to someone **fully pardoned by the State of New Jersey**, this journey proves that redemption is real. **Clean slates are possible.** Forgiveness isn't just a legal term—it's a lifeline.

I was once told I'd never be anything. That the best I could do was survive. But now I stand as a man who has **been to hell and made it home**, who built a new path, who mentors others to walk it too. I've turned pain into power, silence into a story, and shame into service.

Every chapter, every trial, every record that survived the fire—they all remind me that **we are not defined by what we've done, but by what we choose to become**.

I'm now building. In business. In faith. In family. And in legacy.

To the dreamers who've been delayed but not denied—this is your sign.

To the wrongly judged, the deeply wounded, the ones trying to put the pieces back together—you're not alone.

To the ones who still carry the soundtrack of their youth in crates and memories—you know exactly what I mean when I say: **it's not over**.

We were never just statistics. We are stories.

We are survivors.

We are a restoration in progress.

So I leave you with this: Don't just turn the page. Start a new one.

Because if I can rise, **you can too.**—Hugh Carter

QR CODE & RESOURCE
GALLERY

🎵 1. Apple Music Playlist

Title: 45s Old School Jams
Link: https://music.apple.com/
us/playlist/45s-old-school-
jams/pl.u-r2yBBYBFjAgWqM

🌐 2. Reyena LLC

Link: reyena.org

🏠 3. 2Souljiers LLC

Link: www.2souljiers.com

📘 4. Book Website or Amazon Page

Link: [https://www.hughlcarter.com] or
Amazon sales page link

DAV.org

Legion.org

Reyena.org

2Souljiers.com

Facebook Divine Restoration Worship Center

Apple Music - We Can Do It

Apple Music - Open Your Mind

YouTube - Mugh Cool Outro Video

YouTube - Cool Mugh Performance

HUGH CARTER
PUBLISHING LLC

I AIN'T GOIN' TO JAIL PARDON ME?
A True Story of Survival, Redemption & a Second
Chance

BOOK SUMMARY

FROM THE STREETS OF TRENTON TO THE HALLS OF JUSTICE, THIS IS THE TRUE
STORY OF A MAN WHO FOUGHT FOR HIS LIFE, HIS FREEDOM, AND HIS FUTURE.

After surviving incarceration, addiction, loss, betrayal, and a broken system,
Hugh Carter didn't just walk away—he stood up.

With nothing but grit, faith, and a mind full of blueprints, he battled back
against the odds: filing for a Clean Slate Expungement, waiting out a pandemic-stalled
court system, and finally securing a rare Executive Pardon from the State of New
Jersey. But this isn't just a legal victory. It's a spiritual one.

In I Ain't Goin' To Jail Pardon Me? Carter recounts decades of hard lessons
— from police brutality and prison bars to reinvention through service, sobriety,
invention, and real estate. His voice is raw, real, and rooted in resilience.

This isn't about beating the system. It's about becoming a better man in spite
of it. If you've ever been counted out, locked up, or left behind, this story is for you.

ABOUT THE AUTHOR

Hugh Carter is a resilient voice from Trenton, New Jersey whose life journey embodies redemption, grit, and reinvention.

A military veteran, inventor, and now a licensed real estate professional, Hugh's story traces a powerful arc—from surviving a troubled past and incarceration to earning a full Governor's Pardon and Clean Slate Expungement.

Through this raw and inspiring memoir, Hugh opens the door to a world few are willing to talk about, capturing the pain of injustice and the triumph of transformation. His voice is unfiltered, unapologetic, and honest—driven by a mission to break generational cycles and spark change.

When he's not writing or mentoring young people in his community, Hugh is building new legacies in real estate and advocating for second chances. His life stands as proof that with the right mindset—and sometimes the right music—you can rise from the ashes and reclaim your purpose.

LEGAL DISCLAIMER

This is a true story. The author has received both a Clean Slate Expungement and an Executive Pardon from the State of New Jersey.

All legal references are part of his personal journey and are not intended to challenge or diminish the full restoration of his rights.

www.ingramcontent.com/pod-product-compliance
Lightning Source LLC
Chambersburg PA
CBHW070911130626
46555CB00001B/88